The Art of Contemporary Woven Paper Basketry

The Art of Contemporary Woven Paper Basketry

Explorations in Diagonal Twill

Dorothy McGuinness

SCHIFFER
PUBLISHING

4880 Lower Valley Road · Atglen, PA 19310

Other Schiffer Books on Related Subjects:

Ply-Split Braided Baskets: Exploring Sculpture in Plain Oblique Twining, David W. Fraser, ISBN 978-0-7643-4652-1

Painting with Paper: Paper on the Edge, Yulia Brodskaya, ISBN 978-0-7643-5854-8

Folding Polyhedra: The Art & Geometry of Paper Folding, Alexander Heinz, ISBN 978-0-7643-6157-9

Library of Congress Control Number: 2020952430

"Schiffer," "Schiffer Publishing, Ltd.," and the pen and inkwell logo are registered trademarks of Schiffer Publishing, Ltd.

Produced by BlueRed Press Ltd. 2021
Designed by Insight Design Concepts Ltd.
Type set in Montserrat

ISBN: 978-0-7643-6213-2
Printed in India

Published by Schiffer Publishing, Ltd.
4880 Lower Valley Road
Atglen, PA 19310
Phone: (610) 593-1777; Fax: (610) 593-2002
Email: Info@schifferbooks.com
Web: www.schifferbooks.com

For our complete selection of fine books on this and related subjects, please visit our website at www.schifferbooks.com. You may also write for a free catalog.

Schiffer Publishing's titles are available at special discounts for bulk purchases for sales promotions or premiums. Special editions, including personalized covers, corporate imprints, and excerpts, can be created in large quantities for special needs. For more information, contact the publisher.

We are always looking for people to write books on new and related subjects. If you have an idea for a book, please contact us at proposals@schifferbooks.com.

Previous page: "Triatom," photo by Ken Rowe.

Contents

Note

Please be aware that the text step number and image step numbers do correspond; however, due to space constraints, not all steps are illustrated. You will therefore have some steps that do not have an image, which is correct; therefore the image numbers may not appear consecutive.

Introduction

Before I became involved in basketry I was interested in many different types of handcrafts, including knitting, crochet, cross-stitch, needlepoint, and embroidery. Then all these fell to the wayside as I pursued my exploration of basketry techniques and materials at The Basketry School in the Fremont area of Seattle. An incredible journey started when I took my first basketmaking classes in 1987. I discovered twining, coiling, and diagonal plaiting—I also began working with natural materials. I was hooked. I could never have guessed where these classes would lead me.

The Basketry School became my home away from home: I enrolled in almost every class it offered, whether I could afford it or not. I was very lucky that my exploration of basketry coincided with the opening of the school, and I was at there at least once or twice a week even if I didn't have a class.

I enjoyed that resource for about seven or eight years until it closed—then, luckily, Fishsticks (another basketry school) opened north of Seattle and my basketry education continued. It was a great experience to have all that exposure to so many wonderful local, national, and international teachers. The various techniques and materials they worked with were in my backyard, so to speak.

Northwest regional basket traditions are rich with intricate Native American weavings and materials. I explored them all while accumulating my own varied warehouse of techniques. I worked with a broad range of materials and started learning and weaving with commercial reed. I then began exploring many of the locally available natural materials—such as cedar and cherry bark and spruce and cedar root—as well as many materials that were not locally available: birch bark, oak, and ash splints, as well as bamboo. I also developed a deep respect for both the art and the craft of basketmaking.

Jiro Yonezawa, an internationally renowned Japanese basketmaker, lived for a number of years in the Northwest before returning to Japan. In this time I was lucky to have the rare opportunity of working with and learning from him. Jiro converted me to intricate Japanese twill weaves and taught me the dedication to perfection that he conveys in his astonishing work.

Color and pattern enticed me into paper when I took a workshop at Fishsticks Basketry School. The class was led by Jackie Abrams, a basket teacher from Vermont, who is nationally known for her works with paper and recycled materials. This discipline was perfect for me, since I approach my design work as if it is a fluid, moving puzzle of pattern—utilizing my considerable background in basketry and unique problem-solving ability.

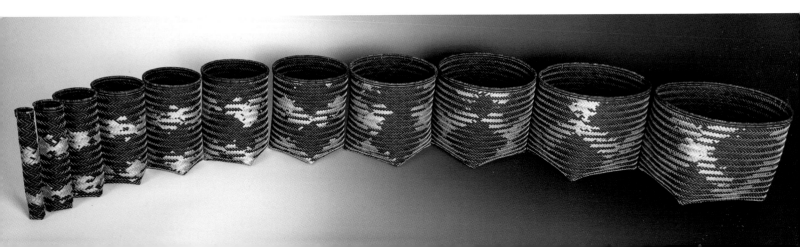

Paper is a very easy medium for working in diagonal twills. Furthermore, the use of acrylic paints allows you to work with whatever color of paper you choose. Best of all, you can cut paper into strips by using a pasta maker! This presented me with the immediacy of weaving that natural materials did not allow. I now work exclusively in diagonal twills to create contemporary sculptural baskets. With each year and basket, I delve deeper into the exciting and puzzling potential of mixing design and color, challenging my mind and hands to ever-more-complex unknowns. I am intrigued by the potential outcome of any new design. The evolution of my body of work is built on taking risks and avoiding the "known." The risks offer challenges, which often lead to new directions. This is the excitement that keeps me working in a repetitive medium.

I often approach my work as a kind of intellectual puzzle, so I experiment with processes and see where they lead. I think, "How will this work out if I try this? How can I achieve this shape or pattern combination? What if I use these colors in this combination and this order?"

Left: "Nearly Twelve." (Susie Howell)
Above: "Twister." Following page: "Citrus," photo by Ken Rowe
Created by Dorothy McGuinness.

I really enjoy exploring math and geometrical ideas such as Platonic solids, Pythagoras's theorem, and Möbius strips, so I am also interested in the constraints these ideas put on a piece. Using literally hundreds of strips of paper at a time, I explore new structural forms not frequently found in the basketry world.

Stretching my twill skills, with all its interpretive possibilities, really engages my brain and stimulates inventive results. Each sculptural vessel emerges, engages, and—of course—leads to more, and more, and more ideas.

In this book I'll review the kinds of paper I use and some that I have experimented with over the years. I'll discuss the various paints that I have utilized and how I paint the paper. I'll explain diagonal twills and some of the many shapes and patterns that can be created employing this technique. Through this, you will come to understand how I use corners to create some of the various sculptural forms I weave, and how I incorporate math, geometry, and color into my designs. Above all, I hope that I will inspire you to take up the challenge of basketry, and that you will find it every bit as stimulating and satisfying as I do.

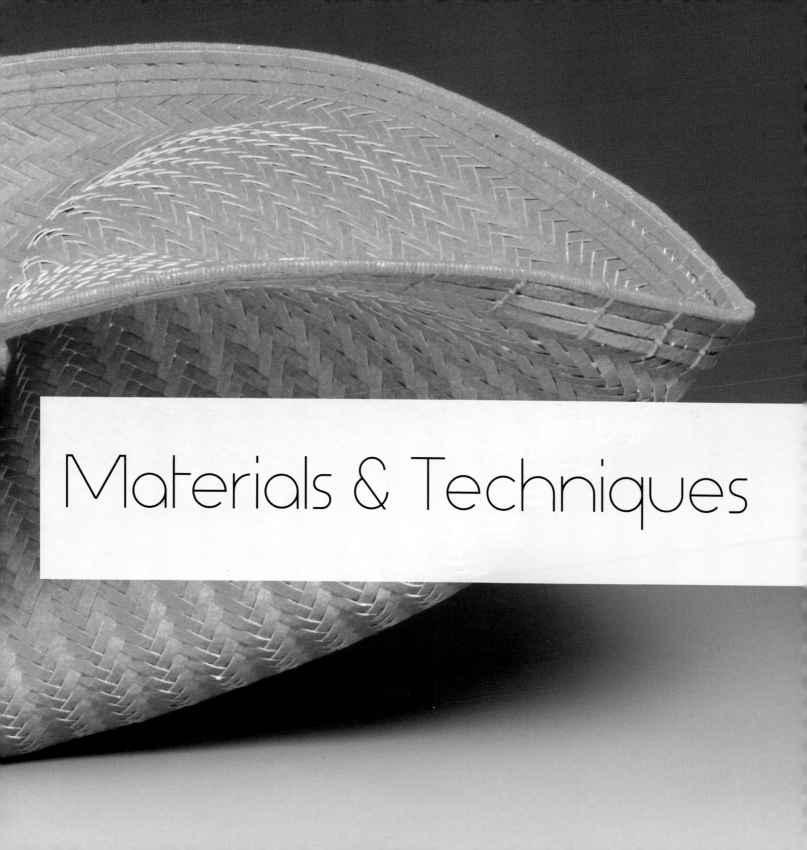

Materials & Techniques

When I began to study basket weaving, I took classes in all types of materials and techniques. I did not weave much on my own—most of my weaving was in a teacher-led class with prepared materials provided by the instructor.

As I grew in knowledge and became more interested, I began to go out and collect natural materials such as cedar and cherry bark, and various types of roots, rushes, and grasses. I did take several classes in preparing bamboo but never became proficient in this meticulous technique—so my teacher prepared all the bamboo I used in workshops. Bamboo, to me, was just one more natural material, but I really responded to the Japanese techniques I learned while weaving bamboo baskets.

I had come to the point where I was trying to find my own voice in the craft of basket weaving, and I was struggling with which material(s) I wanted to concentrate on using. Although I really liked bamboo, I knew I was not really interested in taking the time to develop the necessary skills to properly process it for weaving fine baskets. Also, acquiring quality raw bamboo materials was either very difficult or very expensive.

At this point I worked primarily in cedar and cherry bark. These were locally available materials that could be harvested and utilized in baskets by using various techniques. They were also materials I had a lot of experience using. I particularly explored cedar bark for use in diagonal twills but was less than satisfied with the results. With natural materials you have to go out and collect them, then let them dry and cure from six months to a year. Next, you have to soak the materials in water to make them pliable, and some also require the process of mellowing. After this, you need to prepare the material to the proper

width and thickness, and when you have all the materials prepped, then you can finally start weaving a basket. It's a long, drawn-out process.

In the year 2000, I took a class from Jackie Abrams about how to use watercolor paper painted with acrylics for weaving baskets, and I finally found my medium of choice! I have never looked back, discarding other materials to work exclusively with paper.

With watercolor paper, I have only a trip to my local art store to buy my supplies of paper and paint. There's a minimum of preparation: It requires no soaking, no buckets of water, and no interminable mellowing of materials for hours (or even days). Just paint the paper, clean up the rollers, and then when it's dry, cut the paper into strips with a pasta maker. And I'm ready to weave.

Many basketmakers I know enjoy the preparation of the basketry materials, sometimes even more than the weaving of the basket. I have always preferred the weaving to the preparation.

Below: "Red Stone Parallax." Right: "Caribbean Urn."
Both created by Jackie Abrams

Paper

After discovering paper, a wide new horizon opened for me. I reviewed all types of paper and even examined non-paper materials in this new context. I've collected a broad range of materials over the years that I've played with or plan to explore in the future. This includes plastic papers, textured and flocked papers, holographic film, and wallpaper. I will try just about anything I think could successfully be cut with a pasta maker. Occasionally, I also use commercially prepared materials that are already an appropriate width, such as wood veneers.

In my primary work, I regularly use Arches or Fabriano brands of watercolor papers. There are several other makes available, but I have settled on these two. I typically use 140 lb. (300 gsm) rough-press, 100% cotton, pH-neutral paper. I have tried bright and natural white papers, both of which work well. I have used cold- and hot-pressed paper that friends have given to me over the years. Although both work, I wouldn't recommend the hot press. The very compressed fibers do not cut well on the pasta maker, and the paper strips are more prone to crack and tear. The 90 lb. (190 gsm) rough can also be utilized, but I have traditionally stayed with 140 lb. paper.

I like to use 20 x 30 in. sheets (A1—23.4 x 33.1 in. / 59.4 x 84.1 cm is probably the closest European equivalent). If bought in bulk, ten to twenty-five sheets at a time, you get a better price per sheet, and if you watch for sales the price can be even lower. I buy mostly from Dick Blick (*dickblick.com*) and Jerry's Artarama (*jerrysartarama.com*), but you should definitely explore other art supply sites for better deals.

When I'm planning a larger project piece than a 20 x 30 in. sheet will accommodate, I buy the paper in rolls. These are usually 44.5 in. x 10 yd. (113 cm x 9.14 m) or 55 in. x 11 yd. (140 cm x 10.6 m), depending on the brand. Arches also has a roll of 156 lb. (253 gsm) that is 51 in. x 10 yd. (130 cm x 9.14 m), which will also work.

I could use smaller sheets and piece the strips together for length, but I would rather do the extra work of painting and cutting into strips a large sheet of paper and handling the longer strips, as opposed to the time to piece each strip. I find the piecing interruption interferes with the rhythm of weaving. I do have to piece occasionally if a weaver breaks or I somehow miss equaling up the length of a strip at the beginning.

Sheets of various painted papers

Paint

I enjoy the creative process of being able to play with color and texture, using the broad range of acrylic paints and mediums that are now available. The wide variety gives a range of properties: heavy body, liquid, mat, and satin sheens; also, metallics and paints that iridize in color depending on the angle of the light. In addition there are powdered products that you can add to paint to create different effects. There are solar paints, 3-D paints, and acrylic inks. I am sure there are many others that I just have not discovered.

I have never used actual watercolor paint. It is possible, but an appropriate protective finish would have to be used over it. If paint is applied to plastic, realize that plastic-on-plastic will not be permanent without a varnish applied over the paint.

If you really get into playing with mixing paint, I would suggest Golden's paint mixer on the company website (*www.goldenpaints.com/mixer*). It allows you to play with up to four different paints in an almost infinite number of combinations to see how the colors interact. They also include a helpful tint range on the side.

Never feel you have to start out using some of the more expensive brands of paint. There are many makes that also have fine student lines that are much more reasonably priced. Some stores such as Blick have house brands that are also more moderately priced. These brands do not usually have the pigment load that the more expensive paints have, but initially you probably will not notice a difference.

Predominantly, I use Golden Heavy Body acrylic paints. I like the Jacquard Lumiere paints and Pearl EX powders. I have also used various brands including Liquitex, Amsterdam, and Nova Color. I have experimented with fabric and decorative paints and acrylic inks.

Jacquard Pearl EX powders

Jacquard Lumiere paint

Golden Heavy Body acrylic

Titan Mars Pale
Mixture
Lightfastness I
Conforms to ASTM D 5098
#1576-2 / Series 1
2 fl. oz. / 59 ml

Benzimidazolone
Yellow Light
PY 175
Lightfastness I
Conforms to ASTM D 5098
#1009-2 / Series 3
2 fl. oz. / 59 ml

Light Phthalo
Green
Mixture
Lightfastness I
Conforms to ASTM D 5098
#1578-2 / Series 1
2 fl. oz. / 59 ml

GOL
A
C
R
Y
L

GOLD
A
C
R
Y
L

Color Theory

A color wheel is an illustrative collection of color that shows how each individual color relates to the other colors. This will help you develop your color schemes. I find this particularly useful when planning my pieces. The diagrams below illustrate the basic techniques for creating color schemes. I suggest you invest in a book or two. Those I've found helpful in my examination of color are The Elements of Color and The Color Star by Johannes Itten, and Color Works: The Crafter's Guide to Color by Deb Menz.

Complementary Colors
Colors that are opposite each other on the color wheel are considered to be complementary colors (example: red and green). When put together, they appear more vivid than when apart.

Triadic Color Scheme
Triadic color uses colors that are evenly spaced around the wheel. Normally vibrant in hue, they allow one color to dominate and use the other two as accent colors.

Square Color Scheme
Square color is similar to tetradic but instead uses a combination of four colors evenly spaced around the wheel. To be the most effective, let one of the four colors dominate.

Analogous
Analogous colors sit next to one another on the color wheel. These colors are in harmony with one another.

Split-Complementary Color Scheme
The split-complementary scheme is a variation of the complementary color scheme, using three colors to create a strong visual contrast.

Rectangle (Tetradic) Color Scheme
This uses a combination of four colors—two sets of complementary colors. To be most effective, let only one of the four colors dominate.

Cold Colors

They give an impression of calm and create a soothing impression. They remind us of cold water.

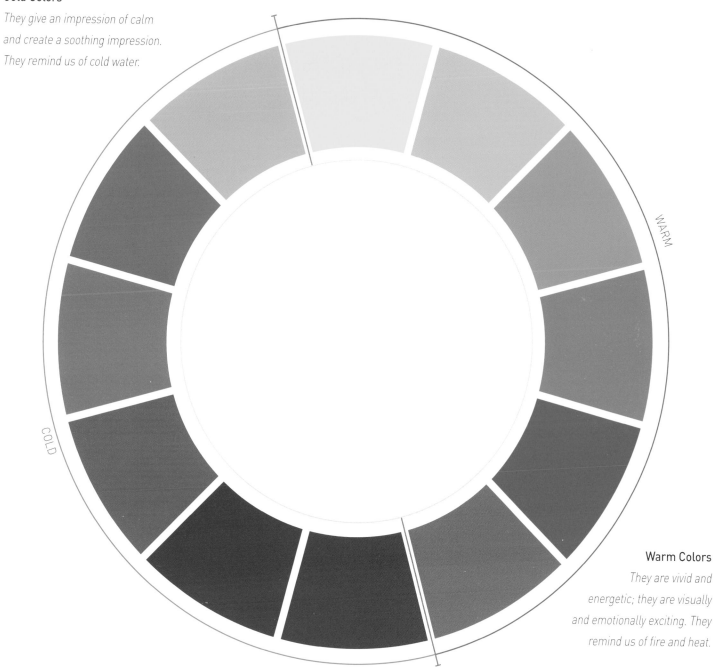

WARM

COLD

Warm Colors

They are vivid and energetic; they are visually and emotionally exciting. They remind us of fire and heat.

Terminology

Twill is different from plain weave (or plaiting), since each weaver (strip of paper) passes over and under more than one weaver at a time. In 2/2 twill, each strip goes over 2 and under 2, and in 3/3 each strip passes over 3 and under 3. In 4/4 twill, each strip goes over 4 and under 4.

O = over   U = under

2/2

3/3

4/4

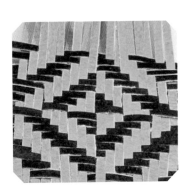

Broken Twill

Broken twill weave is a way to create a continuous weave from the base to the sides of a basket. On the centerlines of the base, the twill will "break" from a continuous twill. On one side of the center the twill will step to the left, and on the other side of the center the twill will step to the right. This creates a place for a corner to be woven so the twill can continue unbroken up the sides of the basket.

Pack/Packing

Packing is when you push the woven weavers together, using your fingers or a flat awl (*see far right*) so there are no spaces between them. This creates a nice, tight basket. You will need to pack the weaving together after every two rows of weaving.

Rim Filler

The rim filler is a quantity of material that sits in the valley between the front and back rim pieces. It is used to cover the cut edges of the basket and can make for a neater finish.

1. A #2 round reed is used as rim filler.
2. 2 x 3 strand braid of waxed linen used as rim filler.

Scarf/Scarfing

A scarf is where the two ends of the reed, used for the sewn and wrapped rims, will overlap. Each end is carved to gradually thin so that when overlapped, the two ends together are approximately the same diameter as the rest of the reed. (See also pp. 96–98.)

Weavers

Weavers are the resulting strips of paper that you get when running widths of paper through the pasta maker. I used 3 mm widths for all these projects except for the simple sewn, cross-sewn, knotted, and lidded projects, where I used 7 mm. The image shows 2, 3, 4, 7, and 11 mm weavers. I used various strip widths in the undulating twill pieces.

Tools

A few simple tools are needed for weaving and finishing the baskets covered in this book. Shown here are the tools that I use the most. You will probably find that your tool kit will continue to grow with the more baskets you create, since you will always be adding to them.

Rulers: I recommend having at least two sizes, a yardstick and something smaller such as a 12- or 7-inch ruler. They will be used for marking where to cut the paper sheets into widths and drawing paint lines. The smaller rulers help with equaling up the weaver lengths on the base.

Scissors: You need a good pair of scissors to cut the paper.

Pasta Machine: Used for cutting the paper into weaving widths. Having several different-size heads is useful so you can make different-size weavers.

Rim Filler: #2 round reed, braided 4-ply waxed linen, and a heavy 12-ply waxed linen are some of the materials you can use for rim filler on a basket.

Painters Tape: I use painters tape sometimes to keep different paints from certain areas on the paper sheet.

Glue: To glue knots in the waxed linen or other thread I use to sew the rims. I use a clear glue such as Elmer's.

Scale: A small scale is nice to have to weigh out the paint for a project and reduce paint waste.

Wire: I wrap a piece of wire at the top of the basket while I sew the rim to stabilize the weaving. Then remove it after I have finished the rim. I usually use 24-gauge copper, but have used steel or brass sometimes.

Foam rollers: I use 3-inch foam rollers to paint the paper. I occasionally use the 1.5-inch roller for stripes or smaller areas.

Knife: You want a good, sharp knife to carve the scarf on the round reed when sewing the rim. I use a Japanese knife.

Weights: I use various sizes of fishing weights to help an asymmetrical piece stand properly. I will sew it into the base of the basket for balance.

Clips: Small, smooth-jawed clips are needed to hold the woven base together as you weave your corners and to hold paper in place.

Awls: A flat awl is the best tool for helping to tuck weavers under when doing a folded and tucked rim, or splicing a short weaver.

Snips & Pliers: I have several different snips to use when trimming up the basket before doing the rim on the basket, depending on the size of the weavers. A pair of needlenosed pliers can come in handy at times needing to grab a needle or end of a weaver that you are having difficulty threading under another.

Flat Toothpicks: Flat toothpicks are ideal to apply the little bit of glue you need for the knots in the sewn rims.

Syringe: I use a 10-milliliter syringe to measure out the water used to dilute the heavy body paints.

18-gauge blunt needles: This is the size of needle I use with the 4 ply waxed linen used to sew the rims.

Preparing the Paper

I begin with a blank 20 x 30 in. sheet of paper and use a 3 in. foam roller to apply the paint to both sides of the paper. Depending on the project, I may paint the two sides different colors (usually), or I may do both sides the same color. Sometimes I will overpaint with one or more colors, utilizing random stripes with a plain or decorative roller. Other times I dab with a Funny Brush, a multitipped rubber tool that can be used for stippling or textural effects.

Decorative foam rollers

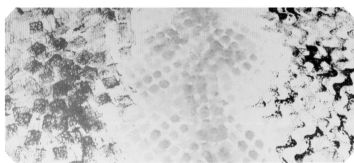

4 in. (10 cm) long Funny brushes

Scale

Pasta cutter

I use a scale to weigh my paint for the specific size of paper I'm using. This cuts down on waste, and if you are doing any mixing of paint colors, you'll be guaranteed to have enough paint to cover the entire sheet without the worry of having to match colors.

When using heavy-body acrylics, I weigh out 11–13 gm of paint for the 20 x 30 in. sheet, depending on how old my rollers are. The older the rollers, the less paint they want to release when rolled on the paper.

To dilute the paint, allow 1:1 weight to volume of water (12 gm of paint is diluted with 12 ml of water). I use a 10 ml syringe to measure the water: but don't add all the water at once. Instead, add 1–2 ml of water and mix the paint in, adding a little more each time until all the water is combined with the paint. If it's a large batch of paint, mix three or four times or more.

When using a fluid acrylic, I use it neat and approximately double the amount of paint by weight.

Medium-body paints will be somewhere in between for weight and dilution: this does not have to be an exact measurement. After you experiment with the process a few times, you'll find what works for you.

Before I had my own studio space, I did not have a scale. Instead, I'd borrow a friend's space over a weekend and paint 20 or 30 sheets of paper at a time. I always had leftover paint from one sheet to put onto the next sheet. I didn't paint for a specific project but would make up a stack and decide later what I was going to weave.

That was then; now I usually have a specific project in mind when I paint the paper. The only sheets not designated for a particular project are ones that I randomly paint after large paint projects—such projects invariably have a small amount of excess paint that I don't want to waste.

Once the paper is painted and dried, the sheets are cut into widths that will fit into the pasta maker. Most

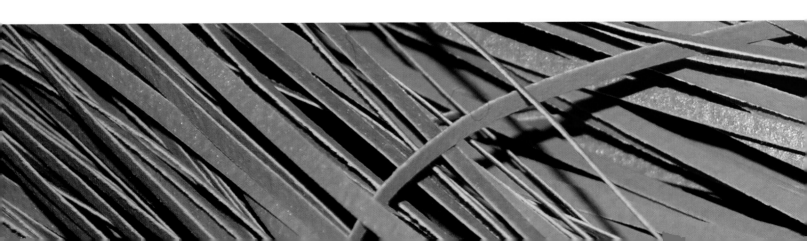

of the time I cut the paper lengthwise; occasionally I'll cut it widthwise. I cut the paper to 4.5 in. or less to run through the pasta maker—I find a wider strip makes it more difficult to turn the crank: the finer the cutting head, the narrower the width.

My usual method is to use a ruler and scissors to mark the first 4.5 in., and then fold the paper over as evenly as I can. I cut a mark for the next width before cutting the paper strip on the fold. I will rule a cutline only if I need to have a specific number of weavers to be cut from the sheet. Otherwise, I just do the quick fold and cut.

After cutting up the paper, I run the widths through the pasta maker. I own both an Atlas and an Imperia pasta maker. I primarily use the former, but I don't think it matters what brand you use. However, it is imperative that you buy extra cutting heads, because they do wear out (usually the gears break because they are plastic). It is important to note that the cutting heads are not interchangeable between the different machine brands.

It's great to have several different sizes of cutters for different-size pasta. I have most of the sizes that are available for the Atlas, and several for the Imperia. However, I don't suggest you buy cutters that make curly-edged pasta, like lasagna. I can cut 1, 2, 3, 4, 7, and 11 mm widths of strip, although I use the 3 mm cutter head the most.

I've found that *fantes.com* usually carries the widest variety of cutter head sizes. There are, of course, other kitchen supply stores that you can order from.

2, 3, 4, 7, and 11 mm widths of pasta maker–cut paper weavers

Strips painted blue both sides with one side overpainted with interference orange

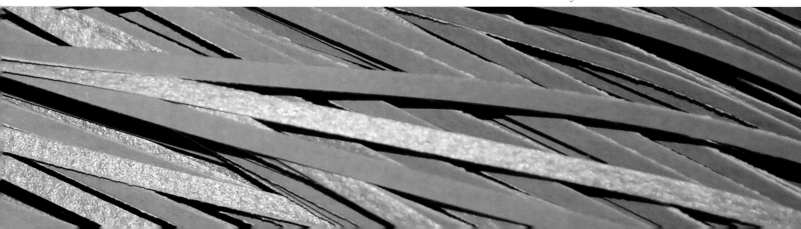

Making Paper Strips

Materials

Paper: 20 x 30 in. sheet of 140 lb. rough watercolor paper

Two different paint colors, one for each side of the paper;
I used a red and a yellow-green paint for this project

First color: 18 gm Amsterdam Carmine
Second color: Daniel Smith Rich Gold Green

3 in. roller
Ruler
Scissors

1. Start with a 20 x 30 in. sheet of 140 lb. rough watercolor paper.

2. Weigh out the paint: here, I'm using Amsterdam Carmine. This is not a heavy-body paint, so I took 18 gm of paint and used 6 ml of water to dilute it. I use coated paper plates (i.e., picnic plates) as my palate to prepare the paint on.

3. Mix in the water.

4. Ready to paint.

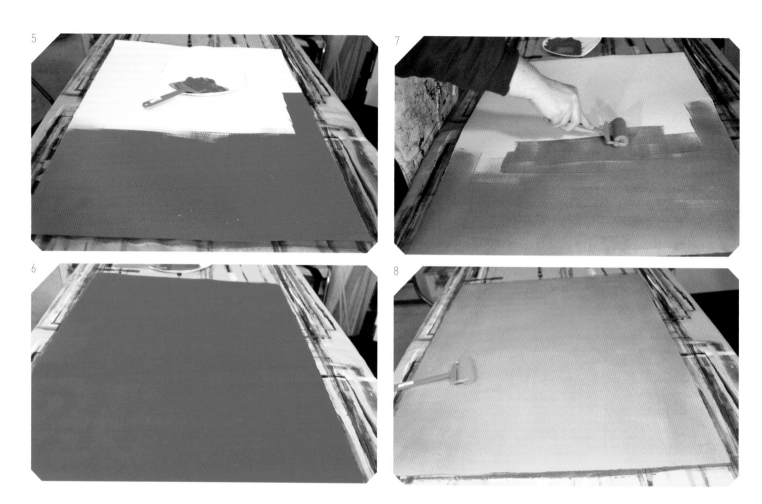

5. Painting the paper.

6. Finished first side. I usually walk around the sheet to look for white spots so I can touch up those gaps. Looking at the paper from different angles can help you find areas that were missed by the roller. The paint needs to dry before you paint the second side. Depending on the temperature and humidity, this can take anywhere from a few hours to the next day.

7. Paint the second side with the second color. Here, I used Daniel Smith Rich Gold Green.

8. The finished second side is left to dry before being cut into widths. If the paint does not look even after it dries, remember it will be cut into narrow widths, and then differences in the paint will not show.

9. Make a small cut mark in the sheet at approximately 4.5 in.

10. Fold the paper over at the cut and cut a mark for the next strip.

11. Cut the first strip off the sheet. To make more strips, continue on as before in step 10.

12. Fold over the second strip and make a mark for the third strip.

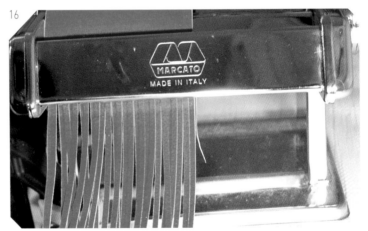

13. The last two strips to be cut apart.

14. Prepared strips ready to be run through the pasta maker.

15. A partially cut strip. Note that some of the weavers are going back under the pasta cutter. You don't want that to continue, because they can come up and around and get caught in the cutters again.

16. The direction of the weavers is corrected so they are all in front of the pasta cutter.

17

19

18

17. Stop just before all the weavers are cut on the pasta cutter, and move aside the waste pieces that are on each side of the strip. The weaver nearest the handle is never the correct width, and the weavers on the far side usually have one or two pieces (or more) that are irregular, so you do not want to use them.

18. Finish cutting the bunch. Grab a bundle of the good weavers and let the waste fall to the side.

19. The bundle of weavers cut from the sheet of paper.

Diagonal Twill

Diagonal twill is used by numerous cultures around the world to create baskets—it is my basketry technique of choice. I really enjoy that once you have woven the base and constructed the corners, you just get to weave. You don't have to stop and add another weaver or add on to your weavers. If I am crafting a larger piece, I use longer strips so I don't have to use overlaps. I use overlaps only when a weaver breaks, or sometimes when I didn't even out the weavers properly and I have a short one.

I like to work in 3/3 twill. I have done some work in 2/2, but it takes rather longer to weave, while the 4/4 twill goes even faster (of course). I don't feel, however, that 4/4 makes as sturdy a piece.

To weave diagonal twill so it's a continuous weave from the base to the sides, you need to begin with a broken-twill start on the base. Standard twills are continuous across the weaving, since the step-overs in the pattern from row to row do not change direction. The shift in pattern is all to the left or to the right.

In a broken twill, the step-overs in the pattern will change directions from one side of the weaving to the other side. This means that on the centerlines of the base, the twill breaks from the 3/3 continuous twill. On one side of the center the twill steps to the left, and on the other side of the center the twill will step to the right. In a 3/3 broken twill, as you weave out the base the 3/3 pattern will break at the centerline with a pattern of 3 Over / 3 Under, then 2O/2U, then 1O/1U. As you continue to add another set of three weavers, the pattern switches to 3U/3O,

2U/2O, and 1U/1O at the center. As more sets of weavers are added, the center-break pattern will switch back and forth. All weavers then continue from the broken center with the regular 3/3 twill.

I always work in sets of three weavers. As I am weaving around the basket, I may insert six weavers at a time on a side, but I always use a number divisible by three. (If it was a 2/2 twill, I would use a number divisible by two.)

The number of weavers that you need for a basic square base will be divisible by 12. Whether you start with a 6 x 6 base (three weavers on each side) or perhaps a 30 x 30 base (15 weavers on each side), because each unit larger is four sets of three weavers (so 12 in total) the complete number of weavers will always be divisible by 12.

One way to check yourself as you weave across the base with a broken twill is if you start with an over 1 on one side, you should end with an over or under 1 on the other side. So whatever number you start with of over/under on one side, you should have the same number of over/under on the other side if you have done the weave correctly.

You have to be careful that you are on the centerline of the base when you weave the break in the twill. You do not want the corners to wander from the center of the base. You want them to stay in the center so you get a square base when you begin weaving the corners.

Project 1: Four-Cornered Square-Base Basket

The four-cornered square-base basket is the first diagonal twill basket I learned to weave. This basket will show how the broken twill is constructed The corners are woven to create a continuous twill up the sides.

Materials

Paper: Enough of a 20 x 30 in. sheet of 140 lb. rough watercolor paper for 36 strips, plus some rim pieces

Two colors, one for each side—I used red and yellow

Clips

Flat awl

Materials for finishing as required

Ruler

Snips

1. Lay out six strips vertically and have six more strips set aside for the next step.

2. Take the first strip and, weaving right to left, go over 3 and under 3.

3. Working in a direction away from yourself, add the next strip weaving under 1, over 2, under 2, and over 1.

4. The third row is under 2, over 1, under 1, and over 2.

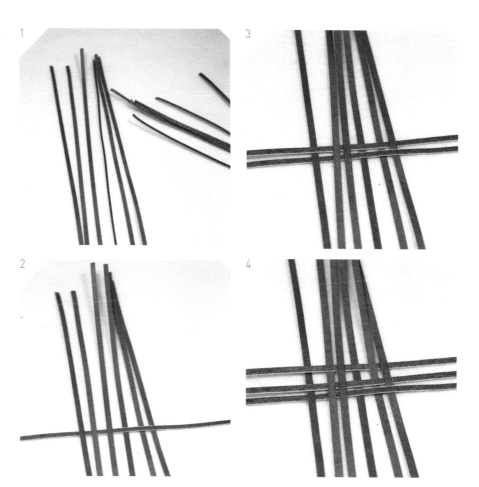

5

6b

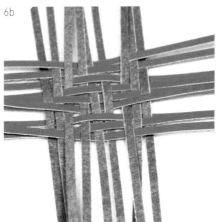

6a

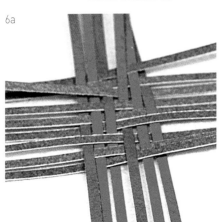

7

5. At this point, turn the work 180 degrees and add three more weavers in the same manner, so you have a square that is 6 x 6 strips.

6. The next set of three will be under 3, over 3; O1, U2, O2, U1; O2, U1, O1, U2 (**6a**). As the base increases in size, it is important to always execute the broken twill at the center, even though it may not look like the center. The first side and the fourth side will be centered, but the second and third will have more weavers on one side of the center (**6b**).

7. Then turn the weaving 90 degrees and weave the next set of three, continuing until you have a 12 x 12 square. You always want the center to be 3/3, 2/2, 1/1, with the pattern weaving out 3/3 from the center break. The twill steps will step over the opposite direction from the center.

8. Continue to add sets of three weavers around the base with the 3/2/1 broken twill center until you have a base that is composed of 18 x 18 (nine weavers on each side of the center). Count to make certain you have the same number of weavers in both directions and that there are no errors in the weave. Turning the piece over can sometimes help you see the

errors. Also, holding the piece up to the light can help you detect errors. If the weaving is particularly loose, I would pack them a little bit, but not excessively tight, since that will make it difficult to even up your weavers.

9. Even up the weavers so that you have equal lengths on each side. You can do this with a ruler or by folding up a weaver and adjusting it so it is the same length on each side, and then using that weaver as a guide to adjust the rest. It does not have to be perfect, just close. The center will not want to pack as well as the outside edges because of the 1/1 twill. The width of your basket base is the diagonal width from corner to corner of the woven start. If your base start is 4 in. across, the width of the finished basket will be just less than 3 in. So remember, the width of the start will be larger than the finished piece.

10. Next pack the weaving. Starting in the middle, gently push the weavers together. Proceed around each side, packing as you go, until you return to the beginning. Check to see if the packed square is the same size in each direction. The center will be a little wider, since the center will not want to pack as well as the outside edges because of the 1/1 twill. Repack if needed to make it square. It does not need to be perfect, but you do want to get it as square as possible.

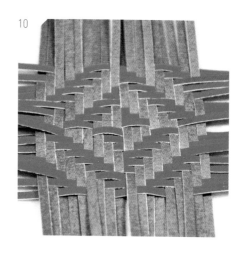

10

11a

13

11b

11. The base is ready to go: it's time to start up the sides. I use small copper clips at the corners of the base to keep everything in place. Then I move them as needed while I'm weaving. The corners are worked from the middle of each side of the base. You will see that in the center, you have one weaver that is under 3 and one that is over 3 next to each other (**11a**). Hold the base in your hands and start weaving the corner by taking the under 3 weaver across the over 3 weaver, and the next two weavers and in (**11b**).

12. Now weave the element next to the first one you wove, and weave it across three weavers and in. This will include one piece on the bottom and two from the side.

13. Take the third weaver and weave it over 3 and in. This time you will have two weavers from the bottom and one from the side.

14

16

15
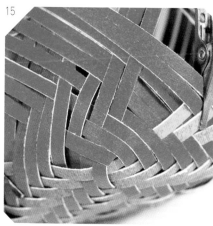

14. Then take the fourth weaver (already going over 3 from the base) and weave it to the inside.

15. You want to take the weavers going in the other direction that were just woven over and weave them over 3 and in, until you cannot weave anymore over 3.

16. At this point I usually take the opportunity to work on shaping the corner a little. I do this by placing my thumb inside the corner and gently pressing it into shape while gently packing the weavers closer together. Do not try to force them into place all at once. Pack the weavers a little in each direction, and fold the base carefully along the line between the corners to start to bring up the sides. You likely will not be able to get weavers completely packed, and they will have a tendency to loosen as you continue to construct the corner. But don't worry about this at the moment.

17. At this time, weave back in the other direction with the outside weavers, again over 3 and in. You should weave back one more time, for a total of three rows. Be careful to keep the weavers in the correct order. Some like to fall to the back or jump in with their neighbor. You will be tempted to continue weaving up to a point, but resist that urge.

18. Work the other three corners in the same manner. You want all the sides to be at the same height and all the weavers on the outside to be pointing in one direction, and all the weavers on the inside pointing in the opposite direction.

19. This is how the base should look. Now you need to pack the piece: especially look at the corners and pack them as well as you can. Sometimes it can help to tug on the weavers a little to tighten them up, particularly the corner weavers. Do not pull so much that you distort the corners. At this point you need to pack each weaver around the basket, from the base to the top in both directions. You may need to do this more than once, depending on how loose the weave was. You most probably will not be able to pack them perfectly. You can pack again as you weave up the sides. The more weaving you have done on the basket, the more the weavers will stay in place.

17

18
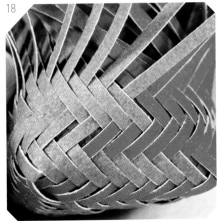

19

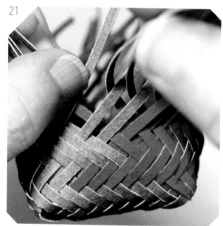

20. When you have packed as well as you can, you can start weaving. Remember it does not have to be perfect. To weave the sides, you take several outside weavers in your hand—if the outside weavers are pointing to the left, you pick them up with your right hand (or your left hand if pointing to the right). You will weave in the opposite direction to where the weavers are pointing. If they are to the left, you will weave to the right, and vice versa. Pick up a weaver in your right hand from the inside and drop one weaver from your left hand from the outside; take this over three weavers on the inside and in under the piece in your right hand.

21. Then pick up the next weaver to the left with your right hand and drop the next weaver from the left over 3 and beneath the right-hand weaver. Continue this action all around the basket until you have returned to the beginning. As you are weaving around, you will need to adjust your hands and drop and pick up bunches of weaver as you go along.

22. After you have done one row, all the outside weavers should be inside and vice versa. If the weaving does not end evenly—e.g., the last weaver is only going over 2—it probably means you have an error in your weaving, where you went over 4 or 2 instead of 3. You need to check the basket to find the error. Sometimes weavers will double up or fall to the inside or just get missed. The most likely times for me to make an error in the weave are at the beginning of a row or when I adjust my hands. If you watch as you weave, you can usually catch the error after you have woven only a short way—so you can correct the error quickly and not have to (perhaps) go all the way back to the beginning to correct and reweave the row.

23. The next row is the same as the first, just with the opposite hands doing the picking and dropping and weaving in the opposite direction (23a). I usually stop at this point and pack again (23b).

24. I really work to get the corners packed well and work on the sides. I do this after every two rows of weaving, packing one direction, then the opposite direction.

25. Continue weaving until you come to your shortest weaver—there will be some weavers that are longer. The pieces woven at the center of the base have the farthest distance to weave, so they will be the shortest. The weavers on the outside of the base will be longer, because they have had a shorter distance to weave.

26. **Finishing.** There are various options when it comes to finishing the rim on the basket—as outlined on **pp. 70–119**. Once you've chosen your preferred finish, follow the relevant instructions.

Project 2: Two-Cornered Basket

A two-cornered basket also begins with
a square base, but the broken twill is
different, so there are only two places
where the twill will work up into the corners
and sides properly. This process works up
into a pouch shape.

Materials

Paper: Enough of a 20 x 30 in. sheet of 140 lb. rough watercolor paper
for 24 strips, plus some rim pieces

Two colors, one for each side—I used gray and yellow

Clips

Flat awl

Materials for finishing as required

Ruler

Snips

1. Lay out seven strips vertically, with seven more strips set aside for the next step. Weave under 3, over 3, and under 1.

2. The next piece will be under 2, over 3, U1, O1 (**2a**). Next weave U1, O3, U1, O2 (**2b**).

3. The under 1 should continue to step over to the right with each additional weaver, ending with the last weaver under 1, over 3, under 3 (**3a–c**).

1

3a

2a

3b

2b

3c

4a
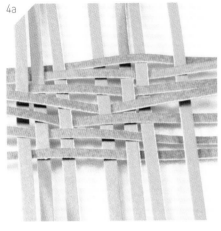

4c
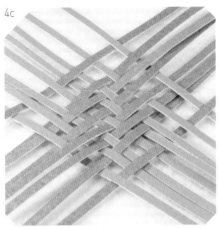

4b
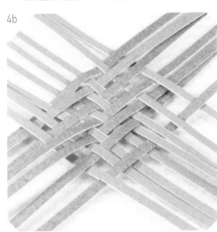

4d

6

4. After adding the last weaver (4a), I turned the piece so that the base is at an angle, with the center breaks of over 1s going away from me. I then added two weavers consecutively, one on the right side and then one on the top edge. The right side should always end as an under 3 (4b). The top piece always begins as an under 1, and they both continue in the 3/3 twill (4c). This puts the twill break moving away from you from corner to corner. Weave a base that is 12 x 12 weavers (4d).

5. If your weaving is really loose, then pack it a little, but not to the final tightness because you still have to adjust the lengths. At this point, even up the weavers so that you have equal lengths on each side. You can do this with a ruler or by folding up a weaver and adjusting it so it is the same length on each side, and then use that weaver as a guide to adjust the rest. If you adjust the weavers this way, you will have more wastage at the end of the weaving.

6. Another way to adjust the weavers can give you two or more rows of weaving at the top of your piece. In this adjustment, at the corner outside weavers that are over or under 1, you take the outermost weaver on both sides and

7

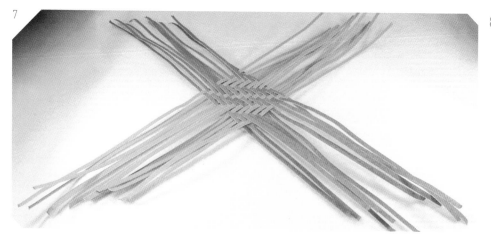

8

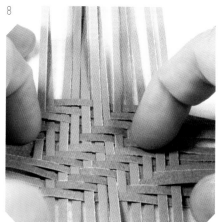

8. Now you can pack the base. Starting in the middle, gently push the weavers together. Proceed around each side, packing as you go. I find it easier to pack in the same direction as the under 1s. After doing one side, I turn the piece over so I can pack the other direction, still working with the under 1s. I'll switch back and forth as I continue to pack. Check to see if the packed square is the same size in each direction. Repack if needed to make it square. It does not need to be perfect, but you want to get it as square as you can.

gently fold it and adjust the ends so they are an even length. You do not want to put a crease in the piece; just get it close to even—it does not need to be perfect.

7. Then do the opposite corner the same way. As you look at the base, you will have long weavers at one end of a side and shorter ones at the other end. You need to adjust all the weavers so they graduate in length between the longest one and the shortest. Again, this doesn't have to be perfect; it just needs to be reasonably close. Do the same in the other direction.

9. The corners on the pouch are done in the same manner as for the square, except you are going to be weaving on a corner of the base, so the angle is more acute. It can be a little more challenging because of this. At the corner there will be one weaver coming out under 1 in one direction and a weaver going over 1 in the other direction. Hold the base in your hands and start weaving the corner by taking the under 1 weaver across the over 1 weaver on the other side and the next two weavers and in.

10. Now weave the piece next to the first one you wove and weave it across three weavers and in. This will include one piece on the bottom and two from the side.

11. Take the third weaver and weave it over 3 and in. This will consist of two weavers from the bottom and one from the side.

12. Next take the fourth weaver that is already going over 3 from the base, and weave it to the inside.

13. You want to take the weavers going in the other direction that were just woven over and weave them over 3 and in, until you cannot weave anymore over 3.

14. At this stage I usually work on shaping the corner. Carefully press the corner into shape and gently pack the weavers closer together. Do not try to force them into place all at once. Pack them a little in each direction, and fold the base gently along the line between the two corners to start to bring up the sides. Tugging on the weavers to tighten them up is very helpful with the two corner constructions because of the acute angle. Just do not pull so much you distort the corner. You are unlikely to be able to get them completely packed, and they will have a tendency to loosen as you continue to construct the corner. But don't worry about this at the moment.

15. Now weave back in the other direction, again over 3 and in. You should weave back one more time, a total of four rows. You'll be tempted to continue weaving up to a point, but resist that urge. When you have the two corners done, you want the weaving to be all at the same height.

12

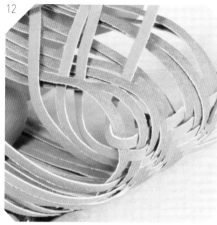

15

13

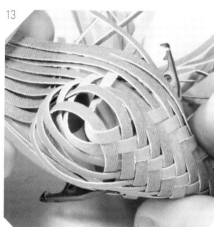

16. Work the other corner in the same manner. You want all the sides to be at the same height, all the weavers on the outside to be pointing in one direction, and all the weavers on the inside pointing in the opposite direction. You need to pack the piece. Especially look at the corners to get them packed as well as you can.

16

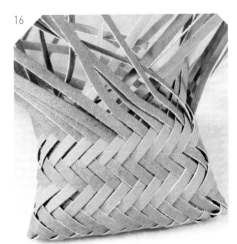

17. You need to pack each weaver around the basket from the base to the top in both directions. You may need to do this more than once, depending on how loose the weave has become. You probably won't be able to pack them perfectly, but you can pack again as you weave up the sides. The more weaving on the basket you have done, the more the weavers will stay in place. Most problems occur with packing on the two edges going around the basket—you will continually have to fight with the weavers wanting to unweave because of the angle.

18. When you've packed as well as you can (remember it does not have to be perfect), you can start weaving. To weave the sides, take several outside weavers in your hand: if the outside weavers are pointing to the left, pick them up with your right hand (or your left hand if pointing to the right). You will weave in the opposite direction that the weavers are pointing—if they are to the left, you weave to the right, and vice versa.

Pick up a weaver in your left hand from the inside and drop one weaver from your right hand from the outside; take this over three weavers on the inside and in under the piece in your left hand (**18a**). Now pick up the next weaver to the right with your left hand and drop the next weaver from the right over 3 and beneath the left hand weaver (**18b**).

19. Continue this action all around the basket until you have returned to the beginning. As you are weaving around the piece, you will need to adjust your hands and drop and pick up bunches of weaver as you go along. After you have done one row, all the outside weavers should be inside,

and vice versa. If the weaving does not end evenly (such as the last weaver is only going over 2), it probably means you have an error in your weaving where you went over 4 or 2, instead of 3. You'll need to check the basket to find the error. Sometimes weavers will double up or fall to the inside or just get missed. The most likely times to make an error are at the beginning of a row or when adjusting hands while weaving. If you watch as you weave, you can usually catch the error after you have woven only a little way and can correct the error quickly. Otherwise you have to go all the way back to the beginning to correct and reweave the row.

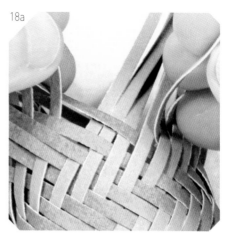
18a

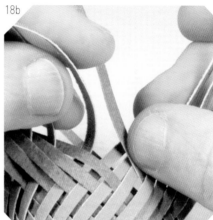
18b

20. The next row is the same as the first, just with the opposite hands doing the picking and dropping and weaving in the opposite direction (20a and 20b). I usually stop at this point and pack again. I really work to get the corners packed well and work on the sides. I do this after every two rows of weaving, packing one direction, then the opposite direction (20c and 20d).

20a

20c

20b

20d

21. Continue weaving until you come to your shortest weaver. There will be some weavers that are longer. The pieces woven on the center of the base have the farthest distance to weave so are the shortest, and the weavers on the outside of the base will be longer, because they had a shorter distance to weave. If you used the graduated-length base, you should be able to get two or more rows of weaving—so less waste. In the image on the left the graduated length piece is on the left.

22. **Finishing.** There are various options when it comes to finishing the rim on the basket—as outlined on **pp. 70–119**. Once you've chosen your preferred finish, follow the relevant instructions.

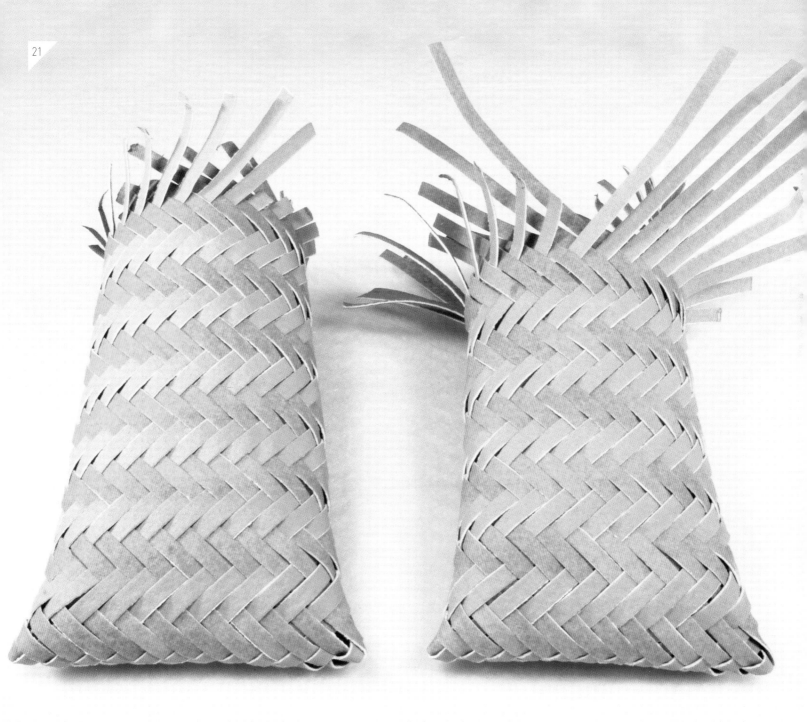

Project 3: Rectangular-Base Basket

The rectangular base starts the same way
as the two-cornered base. This base is
very versatile, since it allows you to weave
something that is almost square, all the
way to a very long, skinny piece—and
everything in between!

Materials

Paper: Enough of a 20 x 30 in. sheet of 140 lb. rough watercolor paper

for 66 strips, plus some rim pieces

Two colors, one for each side—I used black and yellow

Clips

Flat awl

Materials for finishing as required

Ruler

Snips

1. Start with weaving up a two-cornered base, using 15 x 15 weavers. You can even up the weavers using the graduated process as in step #6 and #7 (see p. 49) in the Two-Cornered Basket. Or you can have them all the same length for a square. Place the base with the corner to the right and weave in three pieces, starting with an over 3, and twill to the end. Then add a piece, starting with over 2, and twill to the end, and then add an over 1 and twill to the end. You can see that this is the same broken twill used to make the square base. But the other half is not there yet. The break will always happen above the last over/under one, as shown by the arrow.

2. Turn the work 45 degrees counterclockwise. Next, add three more pieces to establish the next corner and complete the other half of the first corner. You will weave 3 over and then 3 under from the left edge and continue the twill to the end. The center of the break, if done correctly, is always directly above the last woven single on the broken twill bottom—note the arrow. So now from the left edge it will be under 1, over 2, under 2, and woven out in twill. The last piece will be under 2, over 1, under 1, and twill to the end. You want to expand two more sets of three to each corner. It is very easy as you add these pieces to get the corners off. The broken line of the twill is always above where you ended the over/under 1 from the broken twill base.

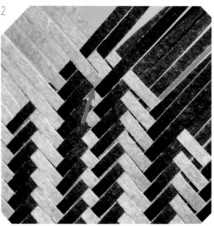

3a

3b

3c

3. After you have added all the corner pieces at one end, turn the base 180 degrees to do the second set of corners (3a and 3b). Go through the same process as in step 2 to add the nine pieces on each side to create the other broken twill corners. Make certain the ends are evened up with the row below. Then make sure the weavers are all well packed, and it is the same width in each direction. Your base should look like the photo (3c).

4. The corners are done exactly the same way as in the square base. Where the corners are on each side, you will have one weaver that is under 3 and one that is over 3 next to each other. This is where to start the corner, just as in section #11 of the Four-Cornered Square Base Basket (see p. 36): the corners will just not be in the middle of the side, but toward one end.

When doing the two corners near each other at one end, I start with weaving them as high as the small section between them that makes up the narrow width of the basket. I will attempt to get them well packed before I weave them to the height of the longer sides (**4a** and **4b**).

5. Now weave the corners at the opposite end. You want all the sides to be at the same height, all the weavers on the outside to be pointing one direction, and all the weavers on the inside pointing the opposite direction. Now pack the piece. Especially pack the corners as well as you can. Sometimes it can help to tug on the weavers a little to tighten them up— particularly the corner weavers—but not so much that you distort the shape of the corners. You need to pack each weaver around the basket from the base to the top in both directions. You may need to do this more than once, depending on how loose the weave is. You will not be able to pack them perfectly, but you can pack again as you weave up the sides. The more weaving you have done, the better you'll get, and the more the weavers will stay in place.

4a

4b

6. When you have packed as well as you can (remember it doesn't have to be perfect), you can start weaving. Weave the sides as shown previously in the Four-Cornered Square Base Basket (see p. 36). As you work your way around, you will need to adjust your hands and drop and pick up bunches of weaver as you go along. After you've done one row, all the outside weavers should be inside, and vice versa. If the weaving does not end evenly—if, for example, the last weaver is only going over 2—it probably means you have an error in your weaving where you went over 4 or 2, instead of 3. You will need to check the basket to find the error. Sometimes weavers double up or fall to the inside or just get missed. I find the most likely times to make an error are at the beginning of a row or when I adjust my hands. If you watch as you weave, you can quite often catch the error after you have woven only a little way and can correct it quickly. If you do not see the error until you have returned to the beginning, you will have to undo and reweave the row.

7. The next row is the same as the first, just with the opposite hands doing the picking and dropping and weaving in the opposite direction. I usually stop at this point and pack again. I really work to get the corners packed well and work on the sides. Do this after every two rows, packing one direction, then the opposite direction. Weave until you get to the shortest length.

8. **Finishing.** There are various options when it comes to finishing the rim on the basket—as outlined on **pp. 70–119**. Once you've chosen your preferred finish, follow the relevant instructions.

Undulating Twill

or the large does not change how the pattern will look on the side of the basket, so this may be a consideration only if you are going to weave a lid. Because you will always have repeats of four sets of three weavers, your sides will always be divisible by 12.

You are not limited to three sizes: you can do more. You just have to remember that whatever size you start with, you need to end with the next size up or down, so the undulations are continuous. If you use four sizes, S, M1, M2, and L, and you start with the S in the center, you need to end with the M1—so 3S, 3M1, 3M2, 3L, 3M2, 3M1 would be the sequence on each side: each side is divisible by 18.

Previous page: "Mountain Swell." Right: "Silver Shoals,"
photo by Ken Rowe.

Project 4: Undulating Twill Basket

Undulating twills are created by using different widths of weavers utilized in a precise order—they are actually a lot easier to create than they look. These two examples are only marginally more difficult to weave than the Four-Corner Square Base Basket. Four-Corner Square Base Basket (see p. 36).

Materials

To replicate the examples shown:

Paper: A full 20 x 30 in. sheet of 140 lb. rough watercolor paper to do both baskets. Divide the paper in half lengthwise and paint each half a different color. I used red and yellow, and I painted the other side red.

First basket requires 12 strips 3 mm wide, 24 strips 7 mm wide, and 12 strips 11 mm wide

Second basket requires 24 strips 2 mm wide, 48 strips 3 mm wide, and 24 strips 4 mm wide, plus rim pieces. Cut the strips widthwise from the sheet.

Clips

Flat awl

Materials for finishing as required

Ruler

Snips

1. The weavers can all be a single color, but the piece will be more interesting if you use two different colors—plus it will be much easier to see the weave. You want one color to weave in one direction and the second color to weave in the opposite direction. The only way to get this effect is by painting your paper on one side half one color and half another. I usually use one of the two colors to do the other side of the sheet. An undulating square base starts the same way as the basic diagonal twill with the broken twill center. The line where the color changes on the weaver is under the center weaver, so you cannot see the color change.

1

2. The first piece used 3, 7, and 11 mm weavers, starting with the 3 mm in the center. This pattern looks like a stylized cross, X, or square to me, depending on how I look at it (2a and 2b). The corners are woven the same as in section #11 of the Four-Cornered Square Base Basket (see p. 36). But these corners can be somewhat trickier because of the size difference of the weavers; however, it's still the same process to work up as in the Four-Cornered Square Base Basket (2c). This size difference gives a very dramatic undulation (2d).

2a

2d

2b

3. It may be more difficult to determine when you have the weaving all at the same level because of the undulations. Looking at it carefully, you should be able to see that all the weavers are at the same level, by checking that all the outside weavers are pointing one direction and the all the inner weavers are pointing the other direction. The small weavers, in particular, like to overlap or hide under their neighbors, so it's easier for the weaving to go wrong. You need to be careful to weave them in the correct order so you do not get twisted weavers.

2c

4. The second piece used 2, 3, and 4 mm widths, starting with the 4 mm in the center. The center looks very much like a circle to me. The pattern becomes squarer in shape the larger the base becomes (4a and 4b).

5. It is important when using a two-color weaver to make sure that the line of color change is hidden under the center spoke line. You need to check that the 3, 2, 1 twill going up the center on each side is the correct color. It is very easy, especially on the over/under 1, to place the center color change under the wrong spoke, as shown in photo 5. The change in color should have occurred under the red spoke to the left of the arrow.

6. The undulations are much more subtle when the weavers are closer in size.

7. **Finishing.** A method of finishing both forms of the undulating basket shown here can be found on **pp. 70–119**, and undulating rims pp. 106-110

4a

5

4b

6

Finishing

There are lots of different ways to finish off the edge of a basket. Which one you choose depends on both you and the basket. All these rims can be done on baskets made with weavers that are 5 to 7 mm wide. The simple sewn, the knotted, and the sewn with wrapped rim piece will not work well on baskets with narrower weavers such as 3 mm, because there isn't enough material on the basket edge to hold the thread.

When sewing the rims, my preferred thread is four-ply waxed linen. It's strong and, because of the wax, clings to itself and holds a knot well. I also use waxed polyester thread when I need a color that is not available in the limited color range of waxed linen. The polyester thread comes in a lot of different colors, but I don't like it as much as the waxed linen. It never seems to have much wax, if any, on the thread. Also, I have to use shorter lengths each time because the thread does not wear as well during the sewing process as the linen. And, perhaps worse, the waxed polyester does not like to hold a knot.

The simple sewn and knotted finish may or may not use a filler piece, depending on your personal aesthetic. The filler is a quantity of material that sits in the valley between the front and back rim pieces. It could be a piece of yarn, larger waxed linen (such as 12-ply), some other cord of the right diameter, a braid of waxed linen, a piece of reed plain or dyed, etc. I usually construct a braid of waxed linen if I need filler for a rim.

I often use a temporary piece of 24-gauge wire at the top of my piece to hold the shape as I'm making the rim (*see photo*). I usually buy copper wire, but I have used steel wire. I find the latter wire feels stiffer than the copper, but both work well. The rim work could be done without the wire, but it keeps the weaving from shifting around or

Previous page: "Lift Off V." Below: "Rippled Saphire," photo by Ken Rowe.

starting to spread out as I work. I remove the wire after I have finished doing the rim. Sometimes the wire will inadvertently get sewn over while working on the rim, but then you can cut the wire and it will slide right out.

Another important consideration is to be sure you have some strips left over when you have finished weaving the basket, to use for your rim pieces. When deciding how much paper you are going to need for a piece, you need to factor in an amount for the rim strips and also account for the inevitable waste in the cutting process. It is better to overestimate than to not have enough to finish the basket after you've worked so hard to weave it.

When deciding how often to sew into the basket, keep in mind that the number of spokes needs to be divisible by the separation you choose. All baskets will have numbers divisible by two, and most will be divisible by three. A two-corner or rectangular base can be woven with numbers that are not divisible by three. Take that into account when making the decision of how many spaces to leave in between when sewing on the rim. You might have to do spaces of two and three or some other combination to make it work out evenly.

4-ply waxed linen

Folded Rims

You need a certain amount of length left on your weavers to do a folded rim. It will form a toothed edge on the basket when finished. The length of your shortest piece should be long enough to go over 4 and under 3 weavers, at a minimum. Longer is better because you will have something to hold on to when trimming the ends.

Materials

Note: The start of this project can be found in the Diagonal Twill section on **p. 32**.

I used the basket from pattern 1 (**p. 152**) to demonstrate this finish.

Paper: Enough of a 20 x 30 in. sheet of 140 lb. rough watercolor paper for 36 strips, plus some rim pieces
Two colors, one for each side—I used black and teal

Flat awl

Snips

Wire to hold the basket while you finish

1. Think of the weavers in sets of two. First take a weaver that is in the back and bring it to the front, behind one weaver (**1a**). Fold it to the front, over on top of itself (**1b**). Take a flat awl and make a space and weave the folded piece over 4, under 3. You will be weaving the piece back over itself (**1c**). You should always start with the weavers from the inside of the basket.

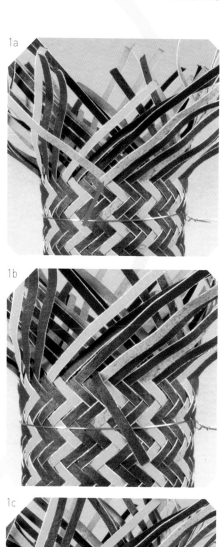

2a

2b

2c

2d

2e

2f

2g

2. Take the weaver pointing in the other direction that is now coming out from under the weaver you just tucked. Fold it to the front, over onto itself (**2a**). Weave the piece over 1 under 3 (**2b** and **2c**). Continue to fold and tuck a weaver in each direction all around the basket (**2d**). You can also do all the folds and tucks going in one direction first (**2e** and **2f**) and then switch to the other direction. I usually do all one direction first, then work the other direction. Eventually the outside of the basket rim will be doubled up with tucking, and you'll need to go under both layers as you tuck (**2g**). Remember: you need to tuck one direction before the second tuck, so that the weaver will be in the correct orientation.

3a

3b

3. After you have woven all around, you can trim the weavers—or if you have enough length, you can do another set of over/under if you like. To trim, I start in one direction and use snips to cut the weaver as close to the basket as I can. I pull a little on the piece I'm cutting, so that it will retreat under the edge of the weaving after I cut it. This does not always work perfectly, and you may see a little bit of the weaver still after trimming it. However, it is not usually noticeable, and you will be the only one who will see it (**3a**). I then trim in the other direction in the same manner (**3b**).

4. The finished piece. You could also create a double thickness for the whole basket by leaving the spokes long enough to weave them down the entire length of the basket. The folding and tucking can also be done to the inside if the basket is large enough to get your hands inside easily. If you tuck to the inside, you will have to weave the layers in the opposite way than if you tuck them to the outside. The weavers on the outside should be tucked first, then the inside pieces.

You could also do the first round of folding to the outside and do the second round of folding to the inside, or vice versa. The colors of your weavers may influence your decision on which way you find more pleasing.

Different color placement and patterns of the weavers in the basket can make the folded rim look quite different. If the paper was painted a different color on the inside versus the outside, that can add an extra design element of another added color at the rim.

4

Sewn Rims

These techniques require the top edge of the basket to have been trimmed to the same height (see p. 80). Then you can use one of the sewing or knotting techniques noted below. In the following pages I show six techniques:

- Simple sewn
- Simple sewn cross rim
- Knotted
- Sewn with wrapped rim
- Multi-rim
- Undulating rim

It doesn't matter what length of thread you use: almost certainly it will get knotted or caught on the clips holding the rim, on the wire that's around the basket (if you use it), or even on the basket itself. To lessen this risk, you can turn the twisted ends of the wire on the basket to the opposite side from where you are working, to keep the thread from catching on them. When you see a knot, stop and untangle it immediately. You don't want it to get tighter and thus make it harder to undo, or damage the basket, or break the reed as you pull it through.

Such frustrations are just part of the process: these issues are not as big a problem on the simple sewn or knotted rims, but they become much more so on the wrapped rims. My philosophy is that it is better to have a little too much length than not enough—and I would rather keep the adding-on knots on the inside of the basket to a minimum. Each basket weaver will need to decide on their tolerance level for tangling and the length of the thread they like to use.

I also recommend that you clip the free thread end to the rim whenever you put the basket down, or work on scarfing to keep the thread taut, particularly on the wrapped rim. The thread can start to unwind itself quite quickly, and you will have to take the time to tighten the threads back up.

Trimming the Rim Edge

1. I use a set of snips to do the trimming, and trim both layers at the same time.

2. You can trim with the outside weaver going to the left or to the right (**2a** and **2b**).

   Note that the simple sewn (p. 81), the knotted (p. 87), and the sewn with wrapped rim piece (p. 92) techniques will not work well for a weaver width that is smaller than about 5 or 7 mm. You need enough crossing material from each direction to keep the rim from coming off easily.

3. The narrower the weavers, the less material there is to keep the thread from pulling out (**3a** and **3b**).

   While trimming, it is important that you pay attention and stay at the same level of the weaving all the way around. When you get back to the beginning of the basket, it is easy to find your cut line is not on the same horizontal. If this happens, you will need to re-trim the edge so that it is all at the same height.

1
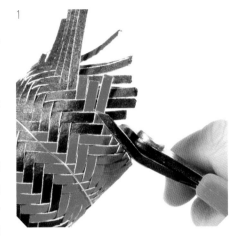

3a

2a

3b
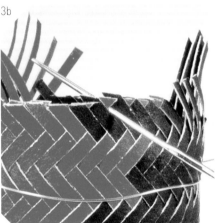

2b

Simple Sewn Rim / Cross Rim

This rim will work only on baskets woven with 7 mm or larger widths, because it uses only one rim piece on each side. The difference between simple sewn and simple sewn cross rim is the double wrap that creates a crossed thread on the rim.

Materials

Note: To get to the stage shown in photo 1, you will need to follow Project 1 (see p. 36), using weavers made with the colors noted below.

Paper: Enough of a 20 x 30 in. sheet of 140 lb. rough watercolor paper for 24 strips, plus some rim pieces
Two colors, one for each side. I used a yellow and a red/white/yellow mixture on the basic sewn basket: solid yellow on the outside, and on the cross-sewn piece, pattern 4 (p. 153).

Clips
Glue (clear-drying)
Needle—I use a blunt-nose 18-gauge
Snips
Toothpick
Wire—24-gauge, to hold the basket's shape
Waxed linen or polyester thread

1. After you have trimmed the top edge, prepare two weavers long enough to go around the basket. One is for the inside and one is for the outside (**1a**). I start them at approximately the same place. Clip them to the rim, overlapping about 1.5–2 in. (or more), depending on the width of the strips and the size of your basket. I usually leave plenty of overlap and will trim the rim pieces off once I have covered the overlap by at least three overstitches of thread on the rim. I sometimes do more, but three overstitches seem to be a good number to be certain the rim pieces are secure. I occasionally do only two when material is short, but never only one. If the rim material is too short, I'll overlap more than one piece to get the length I need, again overlapping enough so that I have two or three overstitches at each join (**1b**). The inner circumference of the basket is actually significantly smaller than the outside, so if you do have a short rim piece, try it on the inside: it may be long enough to use there. If you want to emphasize the rim, you can add rim fillers at this stage (see step 11, p. 86).

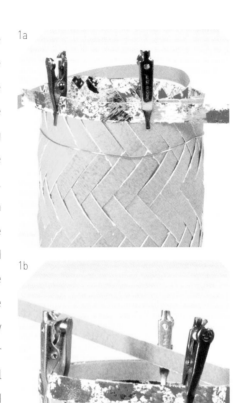

1a

1b

2. You need a blunt-nose needle that has an eye large enough to thread the waxed linen or polyester. I use an 18-gauge needle. If you are using a different size thread, you may need a different gauge of needle. I like to start with about an arm's length of thread. Depending on the size of your basket, you will likely need to use more than one length to sew all around the rim. You can, of course, use a different length that works better for you.

3

3. Take the threaded needle up between the inner rim and the basket and leave a tail of a couple of inches long or enough to tie a knot. I bring the tail up to the top of the basket and then clip it to the left, so it is secure and cannot pull out.

4a

4. Bring the needle to the front of the basket and sew into the weaving, finding a spot between the weavers just below the rim piece, and into the basket below the inner-rim piece (4a). Tighten up the thread. You need the thread tight, but not so much that it distorts the weaving. I usually lay the thread at the same angle as the weaving, but you can experiment with that to get a different look (4b).

4b

5

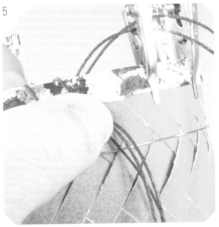

6

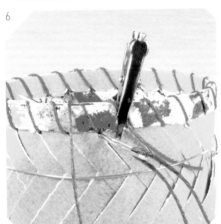

7a

7b

5. Bring the thread to the front again: hold it with your thumb to keep it taut, and sew into the next spot over in the weaving. Depending on how large your basket is, you can go into every spot or skip over one or two. I usually go in every spot for this rim treatment. Continue to sew all around the circumference rim of the basket. If there is a weaver that is sticking up too high, trim it so it does not stick up above the rim piece.

6. Approaching back to the beginning of my sewing, I move the free tail and clip it out of the way to the right of where I started. After having gone all around the rim, I'll sew into the first stitch that I made.

7. At this point you can either knot together the tail end and the working end or continue to produce a cross stitch (steps 8 and 9, *opposite*). Try to keep the knot as close to the rim piece as possible (7a). To keep the knot secure, I like to apply a dab of glue on it, using a flat toothpick. I prefer clear Elmer's Glue, but any clear-drying glue will work. Trim the ends after it has dried. When using the polyester thread, I glue it as soon as I make the knot, since the polyester likes to come undone. To add a new thread, start it just like before, weaving the tail underneath the inner rim piece where the end of the old piece has ended on the inside. Clip both ends to the rim for the moment and continue on with sewing the rim with the new thread. After a few stitches you can tie the two ends off close to the inner rim piece, or you can wait until you are done with the rim (7b).

8a

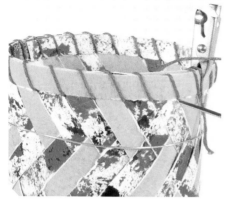

8b

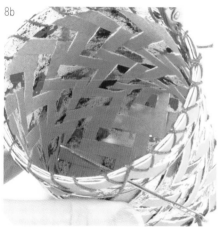

9

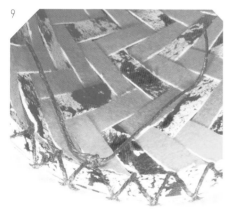

8. Instead of knotting the ends after sewing into the first stitch at the end (as in step 6), you can continue sewing to produce a cross pattern. To do this, start sewing in the opposite direction, going into the same spots front to back as you did on the first course (8a). I usually adjust the lay of the thread as I work, so the cross lies on the top of the rim (8b). If you want the cross more to the front of the rim, you need to adjust your first round of wrapping to lie at a different angle. If there's a weaver that is sticking up too high, trim it so it does not stick up above the rim piece.

9. On finishing back where you started, tie the two ends together, keeping the knot as close to the rim as possible.

10. Compare the rims of the two finished baskets: simple sewn rim (**10a**) and cross rim (**10b**).

11. Rim Fillers

If you want to emphasize the rim, you can use rim fillers. Once you have chosen your filler, add it as you are clipping on the rim pieces (**11a**). To end the rim filler when it's been worked all the way around the basket rim, I push the beginning of the filler between the basket and the inner rim (**11b**), and the other end between the basket and the outer rim (**11c**). Intend to overlap by 0.5–1 in. depending on the size of the basket. I try to be certain that I end them where the sewing thread will be crossing over the overlap, to help keep everything secure. Additionally, I may put a little glue on them to keep the ends from popping out.

10a

10b

11b

11c

11a

Knotted Rims

I first learned to weave this simple little decorative border from a Hmong basket weaver. He was left-handed, so I originally learned to do it to the left.

Materials

Note: To get to the stage shown in image 1 (**p. 88**), you will need to follow Project 1 (see p. 36).

Paper: Enough of a 20 x 30 in. sheet of 140 lb. rough watercolor paper for 24 strips, plus some rim pieces
Two colors, one for each side. I used a yellow and red/white/yellow mixture, and pattern 4 on this piece.

Clips
Glue (clear-drying)
Needle—I use a blunt-nose 18-gauge
Rim filler, I used three-strand braid waxed linen
Snips
Toothpick
Waxed linen or polyester thread
Wire—24-gauge, to hold the basket's shape

1. After you have trimmed the top edge, prepare two weavers long enough to go around the basket. One is for the inside and one is for the outside. Start them at approximately the same place. Clip them to the rim, overlapping about 1.5–2 in. (or more), depending on the width of the strips and the size of your basket. This rim will work only on baskets woven with 5 mm or larger widths, because it uses only one rim piece on each side.

   I usually leave plenty of overlap, and trim the rim pieces off once I have covered the overlap by at least three overstitches of thread on the rim. I sometimes do more, but three is a good number to be certain the rim pieces are secure. I occasionally make only two when material is short, but never only one. If the rim material is too short, I overlap more than one piece to get the length I need; again, overlapping enough so that I have two or three overstitches at each join. The inner circumference of the basket is actually significantly smaller than the outside, so if you do have a short rim piece, try it on the inside; it may be long enough to use there. I used a braided length of waxed linen as a rim filler in this basket.

2. You will need a blunt-nose needle that has an eye large enough to thread with the waxed linen (or polyester). I use an 18-gauge needle. If you are using a different-size thread, you may need a different gauge of needle. Start with about an arm's length of thread to begin. Depending on the size of your basket, you will likely need to use more than one length to sew all around the rim. Use the length that works best for you.

   Leave a tail on the outside, 2–3 in. long, and hold it with your thumb to the left of where you intend to sew into the basket. Do this below the outer rim piece and under the inner rim piece. Sew into the basket again in the same place.

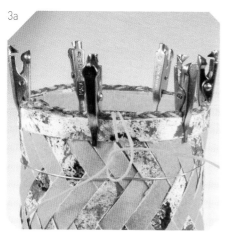
3a

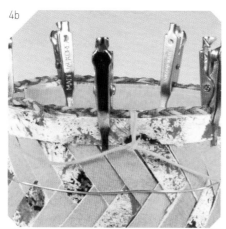
4b

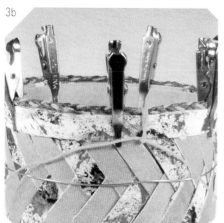
3b

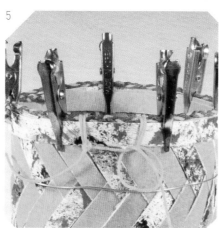
5

4a

3. Bring the thread over the top again and wrap the thread around the trailing tail and into the loop just formed (3a). Pull tight while holding onto the trailing tail (3b).

4. Wrap the thread around the trailing thread again and into the loop formed to make a knot, and pull tight. You want to keep the trailing thread taut as you wrap around it, and while tightening the knot (4a and 4b).

5. Sew into the basket two or three spots to the right: again sew into the same place twice and wrap the thread around the thread between stitches, twice pulling tight each time to make the next knot. Continue doing this around the basket. If there is a weaver that is sticking up too high, trim it so it does not stick up above the rim piece.

6. When you get back to the beginning, catch the trailing thread from the start in one or two knots at the end of the process. You could get away with catching the thread ends in only one knot, but I usually do two just to be sure it is secure. To add on another thread, you'll need to plan to catch the end of the new thread in one or two knots made with the old thread, and catch the old thread in one or two knots of the new thread. I usually secure the knots with a little glue when I am done with the rim.

7. After tying the last knot, take the thread to the first knot and make another knot around it (**7a–7d**). Add a dab of glue on that last knot and the first knot(s) to secure the trailing end and to keep them secure: let it dry before trimming off any excess.

8. The finished piece, with some trimming of the thread still to be done.

6

7c

7a
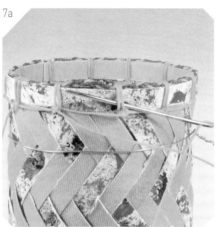

7d

7b

8

Sewn with a Wrapped Rim

The sewn wrapped rim is, I think, one of the more finished and refined rim techniques. It gives the basket a clean, completed look. It does, though, take a little more time and skill to execute.

Materials

Note: To get to the stage shown in image 1a, you will need to follow Project 1 (see p. 36). To finish this piece with a lid, see pp. 111–114.

Paper: Enough of a 20 x 30 in. sheet of 140 lb. rough watercolor paper for 24 strips, plus some rim pieces

Two colors, one for each side. I used a yellow and a red/white/yellow mixture, and pattern 1 on the piece.

Clips

#2 round reed

Glue (clear-drying)

Needle—I use a blunt-nose 18-gauge

Snips

Toothpick

Waxed linen or polyester thread

Wire—24-gauge, to hold the basket's shape

1a

2

1b

1. With this rim, you will have a third element to work with—a piece of round reed: I use #2 as a filler wrapped on the top of the rim. This piece should be several inches longer than the circumference of the basket. Again, this rim will work only on baskets woven with 5 mm or larger widths, because it uses only one rim piece on each side. Take the piece of reed and clip it onto the top of the basket along with the outer and inner rim pieces. Start with the reed to the right of where the rim pieces overlap (1a and 1b).

2. Take the threaded needle up between the inner rim piece and the basket. Secure several inches of the tail by clipping it to the top. Before starting to wrap the reed, check that the inner rim piece is covering the entire top edge of the basket, without any stray pieces sticking out. If any material is showing, gently pull the rim away and trim up the basket edge so it does not show above the rim piece. (See below step 7 in the multi-rim wrapped piece, p. 103.)

3. Start wrapping the piece of reed front to back. I try to wrap about half the distance between the spots that I will sew into the basket. If I am sewing into the basket every two weavers, I try to wrap about the width of a weaver.

4. Sew into the basket below the outer rim piece, between the weavers. Wrap it around the reed again from front to back. Make sure the thread is tight, and hold it with your thumb as you start the next wrap of thread. You want to be sure that the first wrap after weaving into the basket is tight, but not so tight as to distort the basket or break the reed.

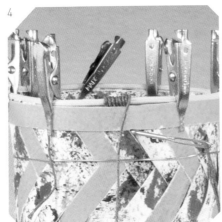

5. Continue wrapping the reed, pushing the threads together with your fingernail to keep them close together and completely cover the reed (**5a**). Keep wrapping until you are above where you wish to sew into the basket again. I usually wrap over a distance of two or three spaces. Sew into the basket again from the front, and start wrapping the reed again. I try to wrap the thread to the point on the reed that the thread will be totally vertical when sewing into the basket. This is not always possible—sometimes the thread leans a little bit to the left or right, but I try to get as close to the vertical as I can (**5b**).

5a
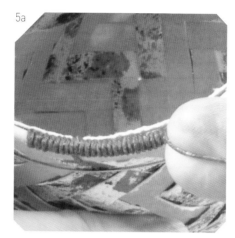

5b
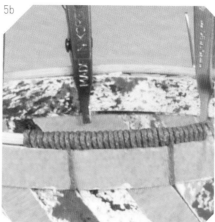

Scarfs

A scarf is created where two ends of reed overlap. Each end is carved—from side to side, not top to bottom—to gradually thin so that when overlapped, the two ends together are approximately the same diameter as the rest of the reed. An extra length of reed included at the beginning makes it easier to hold while doing the scarf, and it gives you some leeway in case you make a mistake while scarfing. You want a sharp knife to do the scarf, since a dull one will just cause frustration.

If you have never carved a scarf, it's a good idea to practice on a separate piece of reed to get the hang of it. Doing scarfs on a basket can be a little tricky, depending on the size of your basket. Rehearsing the process ahead of time can help you get the technique down. The scarf can be anywhere from 0.25 to 1.5 in. long, depending on the size of your basket and your skill level.

6. When you get most of the way around the basket, use a clip to secure the thread so that it doesn't loosen while the reed ends are scarfed. Place the basket on its side, with the opening to the right and the reed at the top of the basket. Start with the inside rim scarf. Take the end of the reed facing away from you and slowly cut about 0.75–1 in. from the end of the reed, and a beveled edge away from yourself. Keep the other end out of the way with your hand or tuck it inside the basket. Don't try to cut the scarf all in one go—do a little at a time, working mostly on the tip to get it to almost feather if possible (6a). Turn it sideways to check if there's a pretty even reduction; even it up to make as smooth a transition as possible from untrimmed to the tip (6b).

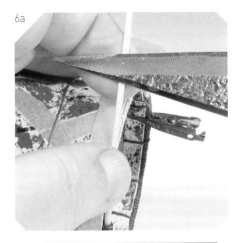

6a

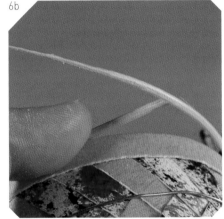

6b

7. For the scarf on the other end of the reed, hold the end next to the first scarf and trim it to length where the scarf on the first end starts. Note where the first scarf tip ends on the uncut reed, and start your scarf on this piece the same way. I sometimes put a small dent in the reed with my fingernail to mark it, but you could use a marker to make a small spot as a reference. Now, turn the basket so the reed ends are at the bottom of the rim, with the un-scarfed end pointing away from you. You want the scarfs to match up as best you can, but they don't have to be perfect. The better they match, the less likely you will be able to tell where the overlap is when you wrap it with the thread.

8. Temporarily clip the inside scarf below the rim so that it is out of the way while doing the outside scarf. Making scarfs takes practice, and you will get better with experience; in the meantime, do the best you can. Leave yourself enough length to work with; otherwise you will have less room for maneuvering your fingers and the knife while doing the scarf. Also, be careful while scarfing: you don't want to cut yourself.

9. After the scarfs are done and are clipped onto the basket, continue wrapping and sewing with the waxed linen until you get to the first end of the scarf. When I get there, I want to be sure the tip end will be well covered, with none of the reed showing. Loosely wrap two or three stitches, then tighten down and push the wraps over the end so the tip will be covered completely (**9a** and **9b**).

7

9a

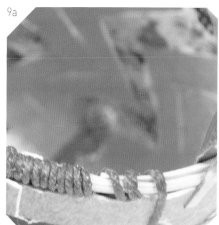

9b

10. Continue wrapping until you get to the other scarf tip—be sure that you keep the thread close to the previous wrap until you have covered up that tip. You will need to push the wrapped threads together from the top, so you don't catch the end of the scarf with your finger.

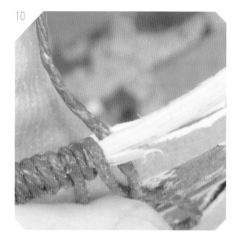

11. After you've covered up the scarf and met up with the beginning wraps, you need to push the wraps together on each end to their respective sides, to get as tight a finish as possible.

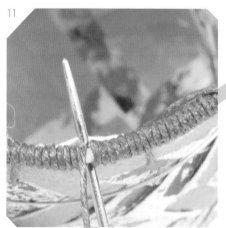

12. After the last wrap, bring the needle down between the outer rim piece and the basket, and tie the two ends together. Try to make the knot ride up under the inner rim piece a little. After finishing the knot, gently push as much of the knot as possible under the rim piece and place a drop of glue on it. Trim the ends after the knot has dried, again pushing as much of the loose thread under the rim. It will not be perfectly hidden, but you will have to look specifically for the knots to see them.

13. The finished basket.

14. Sometimes when you get to the last spot to sew in, you will find that the pattern of sewing is off. There may be two or four weavers between, not the three you have been doing. This means that you made a mistake earlier in the basket and left two or four weavers between sewing in. If I find the mistake was made recently, I may take the thread back to the error and correct it. Usually it is significantly farther back, and I won't worry about it. It will not be noticeable to anyone but you.

13

Multi-Rim Wrapped

The multi-rim technique is the same as the previous process, except you use four rim pieces in total: two on the outside and two on the inside.

Materials

Note: To get to the stage shown in image 1, you will need to follow Project 5 (see p. 124).

Paper: Enough of a 20 x 30 in. sheet of 140 lb. rough watercolor paper for 72 strips, plus some rim pieces
Two colors, one for each side—I used gray and yellow-green.

#2 round reed
Clips
Glue (clear-drying)
Needle—I use a blunt-nose 18-gauge
Snips
Toothpick
Wire—24-gauge, to hold the basket's shape
Waxed linen or polyester thread

1. Clip the rim pieces and reed filler to the top of the trimmed basket. Check the inside rim pieces as you are clipping them on, to be sure they are lying correctly. You clip them on mostly by feel, but they can switch places top to bottom or start to sit on top of one another without you noticing.

2. Start by bringing the needle up between the top inner rim piece (not under the lower piece) and the basket.

3. Wrap the reed from front to back for about half the distance between where you will be sewing into the basket. With two rim pieces, you need to determine the two places you need to sew into the basket beneath and between the rim pieces. These two spots need to be, as much as possible, directly in a vertical line with each other. The second spot is shown with a needle in it: this is the place you sew in and out around the thread.

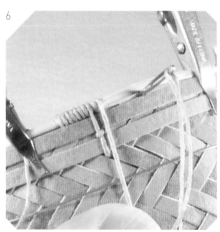

4. Sew into the basket below the bottom outer rim piece and below the bottom inner rim piece. Next, sew from the inside to the outside of the basket, between the top and bottom inner rim pieces, and between the top and bottom outer rim pieces. Try to do so between the weaving right above where you went into the basket, so you will have a good vertical line. You can come out to the left or the right of the vertical thread. I usually come out to the left side of the thread—but be consistent by coming out on the same side each time.

5. Tighten the thread so it is taut, but not so much that it distorts the basket. Hold the thread with your left thumb and put the needle into the same hole it just came out of, across the vertical thread.

6. Pull the thread through and wrap the reed again, front to back, and make certain the thread is taut. Wrap until you are above the next sewing point, and repeat until you've gone around the basket.

7a

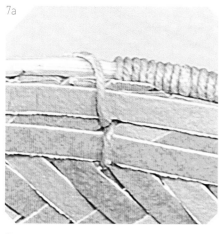

7c

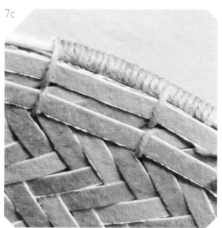

7b

7d

7. Check—before starting to wrap the reed—that the inner rim piece is covering the entire top edge of the basket, without any stray pieces sticking out (**7a**). If there's any material showing, gently pull the rim away and trim up the basket edge so it does not show above the rim piece (**7b–d**). On some baskets you may need to trim almost every time you start to weave around the reed again. At other times you may have to do little or no trimming; this often has to do with how well you trimmed the basket edge. Sewing into the basket can also move the weavers so they are forced up above the rim. Just try to remember to check every time before starting to wrap the reed again.

8. When you get back to the beginning, do a scarf as for the single rim piece following the steps on pp. 96-98. After you have covered up the scarf and met up with the initial wraps, you need to push the wraps together on each end of their respective sides to get as tight a finish as possible.

9

9. On the last wrap, bring the needle down between the top outer rim piece and the basket, and tie the two ends together. While tying the knot, try to make it ride up under the top rim piece a little. After finishing the knot, gently push it under the top rim piece to hide it, and place a drop of glue on it.

10. The finished basket. On finishing, you may find you didn't sew along the same level into the basket as when you started. Unless you began making the error only a few stitches back, I would not try to unstitch it to correct it—you will be the only one who notices the shift in the stitching.

10

Extra Pieces

The multi-rim piece can be made using more than four pieces. You could sew down over whatever number of the outer pieces you have, and work your way back up, sewing around the vertical thread between each piece. You can pretty much do as many on the outside as the size of the basket will allow. If you can you get your hand inside with a needle to do the sewing, you can add on as many pieces as you like to the outside. However, you will need to figure out a way to hold the outside rim pieces in place as you sew. Perhaps use a temporary thread in several places around the basket to hold them, or maybe some painter's tape, which should not damage the paint surface (though I would test that first before committing to it).

If I do a rim with more rim pieces on the outside, I still use only two inner rim pieces. These two are structural, and any more would just be decorative, and that's not needed on the inside. Also, trying to keep the inner pieces in place as you sew between them would be difficult. With more rim pieces you also have to be careful when tightening up the vertical thread that you do not distort the basket, something that is much easier to do with a longer thread.

Extra pieces can be sewn on without incorporating them into the rim work. After completing the rim, you can sew on any extra pieces you like, directly below the rim or farther down the basket. The sewing process is the same: start a thread on the inside (clip it with a long tail to the rim to secure it) and sew to the outside over however many extra pieces you are adding, and then work your way back up, sewing around the vertical thread between each piece. Without the rim, you just move over to the next weaving spot to start the process again. When you return to the beginning, just knot the two ends together with a touch of glue. You will not be able to hide the knot as you can on the rim, but since the knot will be down inside the basket, it will not be noticeable.

Undulating Rims

Rims on an undulating twill basket require a slightly different set of processes. The woven edge is not straight, since it moves up and down with the undulations, so you cannot just trim it off level by eye.

Materials

Note: To get to the stage shown in photo 1, you will need to follow Project 4 (see p. 66).

Paper: A full 20 x 30 in. sheet of 140 lb. rough watercolor paper to do both baskets
Divide the paper in half lengthwise and paint each half a different color.
I used red and yellow and painted the other side red.
First basket requires 12 strips 3 mm wide, 24 strips 7 mm wide, and 12 strips 11 mm wide.
Second basket requires 24 strips 2 mm wide, 48 strips 3 mm wide, and 24 strips 4 mm wide, plus rim pieces. All cut widthwise.

#2 round reed
Clips
Glue (clear-drying)
Needle—I use a blunt-nose 18-gauge
Snips
Toothpick
Waxed linen or polyester thread
Wire—24-gauge, to hold the basket's shape

Broad Weaver Undulating Rim

1. Start by trimming off the top near where you think you want the rim. Then take a waste strip and clip it to the basket as level as possible, using the repeat in the weave to keep the strip as a guide. Choose a spot on the basket to start, and find that same area in the weave as you go around the basket clipping on the strip. It will not be perfect, but it will still be fairly close.

2. Next, take a marker and draw a line all along the top of the basket, using the strip as a guide. Use a waste strip, because it's really easy to make a stray mark on it while drawing the line on the basket. Be careful not to accidently make a stray mark below the strip as well. Remove the strip and cut along the line to trim up the rim.

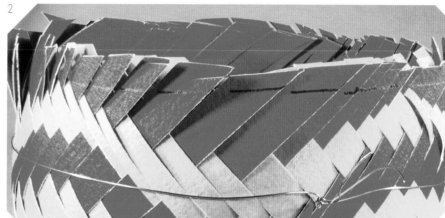

3. I use the largest size weaver from the undulation for the rim pieces. On a basket with a large weaver of 5 or 7 mm wide or larger, I use just one piece each for the inside and outside.

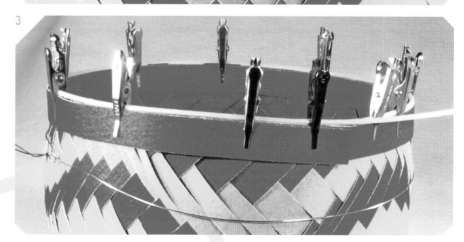

4. This is a wrapped rim using a piece of reed. But sewing into the basket to finish the rim on an undulating basket is not as straightforward as on a conventional twill rim. You need to find places where you can insert the needle between the weavers and still be close to the bottom edge of the rim piece. After you find a spot that will work, you need to determine the next place along the basket that will work. This could be one, two, three, or more weavers apart. These places will not neccesarily be at uniform spots. The weaving pattern repeats itself around the basket, so once you have established the best places to do the sewing, you should repeat the same sewing pattern in each section. The large undulation piece repeats four times around the basket. Counting the yellow spokes, I sewed between 2, 2, 2, 1, 1, 1, and 3 spokes (12 in total). I repeated this pattern three more times around the basket.

5. The finished piece.

Narrow Weaver Undulating Rim

1. Even on a basket where the strips are close together in width, I still use the process of marking the rim height with a scrap piece of paper.

2. When the larger weaver is less than 5 mm wide, I use two pieces together but treat them as one unit—one above the other—as rim pieces on the inside and the outside of the basket. I would not normally use two pieces together this way, because I find that one piece usually wants to slide under the other. So I rarely use it in other baskets. With undulating twills, it is the easiest way to construct the rim when using narrower weavers.

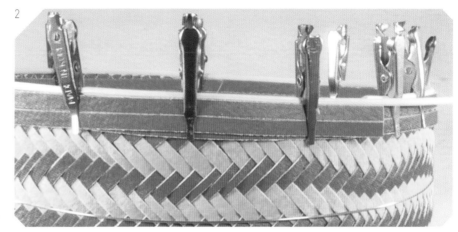

3. You also could plan ahead and cut wider pieces for the rim when using smaller widths in your undulation. For this basket with narrower weavers, I sewed between three, four, and five yellow spokes (12 total) and repeated it eight times around the basket.

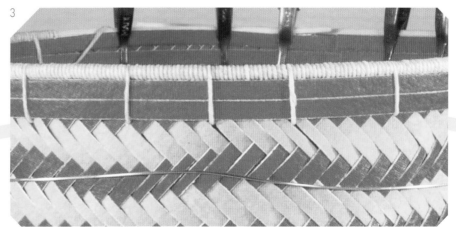

4. It is important to check inside the basket before you start wrapping the reed each time. The undulations make it difficult to clip a clean, level rim edge. It is more likely that there will be areas of the basket showing above the inner rim piece that will need to be trimmed. If I see material showing, I gently pull the rim away and trim up the basket edge so it does not show above the rim piece. See step 7 of the multi-rim piece on **p. 103** and photos 7a–c. The finishing is the same as for other sewn and wrapped borders. You will need to scarf the reed and tie off the thread under the inner rim piece, as shown on **pp. 96–98.**

5. The finished basket.

5
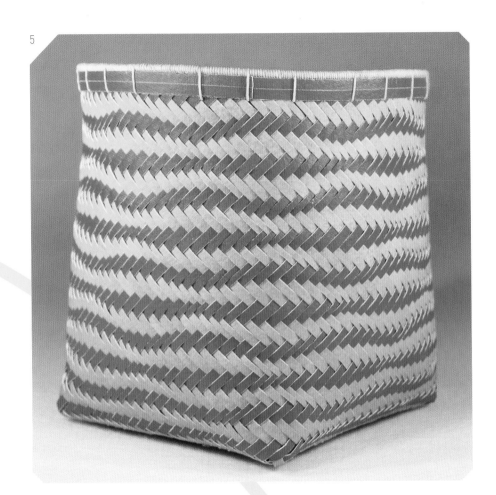

Right: "Licorice," photo by Ken Rowe.

Lids

Another way of finishing a basket is to make a lid for it. Making a lid uses the same processes as making the basket you want to put it on. You can make the lid the same depth as the bottom piece and so cover the whole basket. The lid can also be constructed with a shallow rim and just cover an inch or two of the base basket or anywhere in between.

Materials

Note: This lid covers the piece made earlier in the sewn and wrapped rim piece (see pp. 92–99).

Paper: Enough of a 20 x 30 in. sheet of 140 lb. rough watercolor paper for 24 strips, plus some rim pieces

Two colors, one for each side. I used a yellow and red/white/yellow mixture, and pattern 1 on the piece and the cross sewn rim.

#2 round reed

Clips

Needle—I use a blunt-nose 18-gauge

Snips

Waxed linen or polyester thread

Wire—24-gauge, to hold the basket's shape

1a

1. I recommend that you do not rim either piece until you have both the lid and bottom basket done (**1a**). You want to make certain the lid will fit onto the basket. You can test the fit, though not perfectly without the rims. You can trim the rims close to what you want, and put the lid carefully on the basket. Take into consideration that the rim pieces, the thread, and the rim filler will take up some space as well on both the basket and lid. As you can see in photo **1b**, the basket is too big, and the lid fits inside it at this point.

1b

2. If you need to do so, you can make the bottom basket a little smaller at the top by gently pushing the weaving on the basket together or up with your hands. The wire can help with tightening the top. You can distort a basket quite a bit by doing this—but there's a downside. It can make the process more difficult when sewing into the basket for the rim if you push it too far (2a). You may need to retrim the edge after this to even up the edge. Photo 2b shows that the basket mouth is smaller now, but it is still not small enough for the lid to fit.

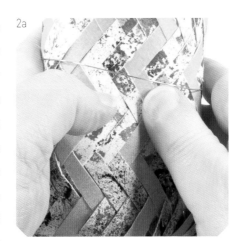

2a

2b

3. Shaping the bottom is usually enough to get a lid to fit. If you did a particularly tight weave on the lid, you can make it a little bit bigger by pushing down and out from the rim—it might loosen the weave up a bit but should not be so severe as to distort the basket (**3a**). You may need to loosen the wire a bit to let it spread. After manipulating both the basket and the lid, I was able to fit the lid onto the basket (**3b**). Usually you do not need to do more than tighten up the basket mouth to get the lid to fit.

4. The best fit is when the basket can be turned over and the lid does not immediately fall off. This can take some practice to get right. If the lid is too tight, it can be difficult to get on and off—this can be damaging to the basket and the rim. If all else fails, you can weave another lid and weave it a little looser. Photos **4a** and **4b** shows the finished piece with and without the lid.

3a
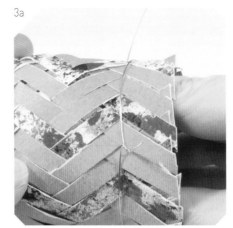

4a
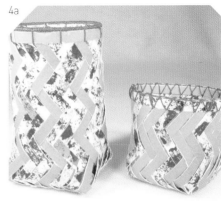

3b
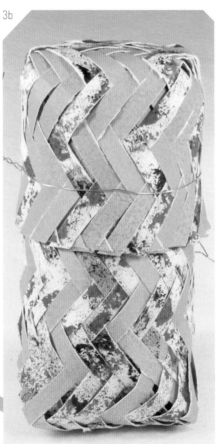

4b

Glued Rims

Many of my pieces do not have uniform
rims—they go in and out or bend and turn.
A piece of wire, therefore, will not work
to secure the trimmed rim until I can get
the rim pieces and reed filler clipped on.
In these cases, I make certain the piece is
well packed, and I will clip the convoluted
rim very well, using many more clips than I
probably need.

Materials

Note: This infinity project is piece 2 made in the Multiple Starts, **pp.**
150–151.

Paper: Enough of a 20 x 30 in. sheet of 140 lb. rough watercolor paper
for 252 strips approximately 7 in. long, plus some longer rim pieces.
Two colors, one for each side—I used a red/orange/yellow mixture on
one side and black on the other.

Clips
Acrylic matte medium
Needle—I use a blunt-nose 18-gauge
Snips
Toothpick
Waxed linen or polyester thread
Wire—24-gauge, to hold the basket's shape

"Zipper Dance," photo by Ken Rowe.

1. This infinity piece it is not too convoluted, but a wire would not work to secure it. Luckily I didn't have to use very many clips while I glued the rim edges.

2. Dilute acrylic matte medium with water, somewhere in the ratio of 1:5, and mix it well. I don't measure, so each time it is probably a slightly different concentration. Then take a paintbrush and paint the diluted medium all along the area where the edge is going to be trimmed. Paint the medium to a width of approximately 0.5–1 in. at the most. Do this all around the basket, both inside and out (**2a** and **2b**).

3

3. Let this dry completely, and then you can trim up the edge
    and clip on the rim pieces without worrying that the basket
    will start to loosen up.

4

4. When clipping on the rim to a sharp curve, you need to be careful not to break the reed. I like to slowly form the reed to the curve, using lots of clips, adding them one at a time as the reed is eased around and into place. More clips are better than fewer! Also try to place the overlap scarf of the reed on as straight a section of the rim as possible. You do not want to be trying to wrap a scarf when forming it around a sharp curve at the same time. The piece is with one set of rim pieces attached.

This process is not foolproof. You still have to be careful not to put too much strain on the piece until you get it sewn. The matte medium can also make it harder to get the needle through the weaving, so you might have to work a little more to get it between the weavers.

5. The finished piece.

"Ocher Infinity"

Structures

Asymmetry

For asymmetric baskets I use a different number of sets of three weavers on each side of the basket base. You would think that you'd just get a base that was perhaps rectangular or maybe a rhombus, but interesting things happen when you don't use the same numbers of weavers on each side. The piece may no longer sit flat, but with corners flying up in the air—sides may not go up straight but may tilt off to one side. When I construct a piece using asymmetrical corners, unless I have done the same design before, I am never certain exactly how they will turn out. I don't know whether they will stand on their own or will need some intervention to make them work.

Previous Page: "Satellite."
Right: "Tilt," photo by Ken Rowe.

Project 5: Baskets with a Four-Cornered Base

The process of creating an asymmetric basket lends itself to a great number of variations. Just adding one more set of three weavers to one side can change the look of a piece. It can also be used with undulating twills: you just need to remember to use a complete set of the different-sized weavers when you add more to a side.

The four pieces shown here show different approaches to the four-cornered base.

Piece 1

Materials

Paper: Enough of a 20 x 30 in. sheet of 140 lb. rough watercolor paper for 72 strips, plus some rim pieces

Two colors, one for each side—I used gray and yellow-green

Clips

Fishing weight

Flat awl

Materials for finishing as required

Ruler

Snips

1. This piece uses a total of 72 weavers. They can be the same color, two colors, or half- and-half colors. Weave a basic four-cornered basket 18 x 18 across, nine weavers on each side, or three sets of three. Weave two more sets of three weavers on one side (six pieces). On the next side, weave four more sets of weavers (12 pieces). On a third side, weave six more sets of weavers (18 pieces). You now have a base that is 30 x 42 pieces, 9, 15, 21, and 27 weavers on each side. The arrow shows the center of the broken twill.

1

2. Weave up the corners and you'll see that the base will not sit flat (**2a**). Continue weaving up the sides. When you get to the top, you will probably find that the basket will not sit up at all but wants to lie on its side. This piece did not want to sit up, so I temporarily placed a weight in it. I usually try to get the basket to sit by playing with the base a little. Sometimes just creasing the edges well will help the piece to sit up, but sometimes it won't! (**2b**).

3. The weight distribution in asymmetric pieces is something you have to consider when weaving them, so that they will sit upright on their own or with the aid of a weight sewn into the base. Sometimes, trimming the piece down several inches can change the weight distribution enough so it will sit. If not, or

2b

2a

if you like the height of the piece, you can use a weight in the base to balance out the mass. I use fishing weights that you can get in the fishing tackle department of a sporting goods store. They come in a range of sizes and shapes and can weigh less than a gram to over 8 oz. or more. Helpfully, they usually have a hole that you can sew through. I tend to buy small to medium, round or bullet shapes. Be sure that your threaded needle can go through the hole when using a weight. If not, sometimes you can manage to get just the thread through the hole.

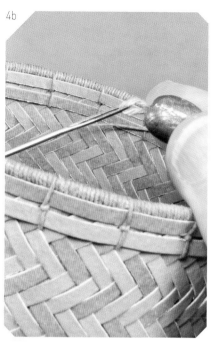

4. When sewing in a base weight, you need to determine where it needs to be placed to make the basket stand. There can be more than one location that will allow the piece to stand, and sometimes in different configurations. Then take a long thread and put a needle on each end and sew into the basket base where the weight needs to be attached (4a). Next, thread the weight onto a needle and let it drop down into the basket. Remove the needles and tie a knot in the thread. If the basket is large enough to get your hands into, this is an easy process (4b).

5. If the basket is small, then you need a long length of thread and needlenose pliers to tie the knot. After tying the first half of the knot, use the needlenose pliers to grab one thread, and while you hold on to the other thread, tighten the knot as close to the weight as you can. You may need to readjust where the plier is holding the thread to get it tight. Do the same process again with the second half of the knot, using the pliers to tighten it up so the weight is secured (5a). Then put some glue on the knot and trim the ends after it dries. Here I placed the weight so that it tilts to one side (5b).

6. To finish this piece I used a multi-rim wrap.

Pieces 2 and 3

Materials

Paper: Enough of a 20 x 30 in. sheet of 140 lb. rough watercolor paper for 36 strips, plus some rim pieces for both piece 2 and 3.

Two colors, one for each side—I used red and a yellow-green.

Clips

Fishing weight for one

Flat awl

Materials for finishing as required

Ruler

Snips

1. These two pieces started with a base of 3, 3, 9, and 21, or 12 x 24 across. The arrows show where the center of the broken twill is (1a and 1b).

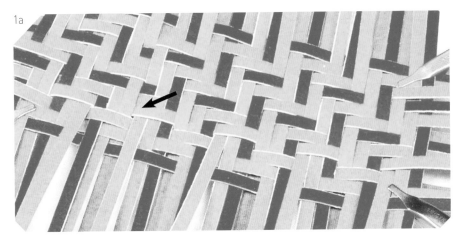

1a

1b

2

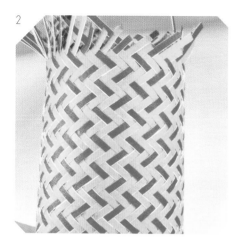

3c

3a

3b

2. When woven to their full height, neither one would stand on its own.

3. The taller piece required about 1.5 in. cut off the top and still needed a weight to stand (3a and 3b). The other required approximately 2 in. cut off the top, which allowed it to stand on its own without a weight in the bottom (3c).

4. **Finishing.** There are various options when it comes to finishing the rim on the basket—as outlined on **pp. 70–119**. Once you've chosen your preferred finish, follow the relevant instructions.

Piece 4

Materials

Paper: Enough of a 20 x 30 in. sheet of 140 lb. rough watercolor paper for 60 strips, plus some rim pieces Two colors, one for each side—I used black and a blue/pink/white mix.

Clips

Flat awl

Materials for finishing as required

Ruler

Snips

1. This rectangular piece uses a total of 60 weavers. It starts with a two-cornered base that is 12 x 12, with two added sets of three weavers for each corner. Another two sets of three weavers were added on each corner at just one end of the base. The corners are marked with arrows. The base is 30 x 30 weavers.

2. When woven up, this basket has a flat base, but the sides do not go up straight (2a). If there had been a larger difference between the numbers of weavers at the two end corners, it would have leaned even more (2b).

1

2a

2b

3. **Finishing.** There are various options when it comes to finishing the rim on the basket—as outlined on pp. 70–119.

Once you've chosen your preferred finish, follow the relevant instructions.

Stair Steps

I discovered this weave several years ago. I like to weave long strips of this technique and weave the ends together to create sculptural forms. The extra corners give the weaving some structural integrity that allows for some of the sculptural shapes I like to create. If I tried weaving some of the shapes I construct with just plain, flat pieces, the sculptures would not stand but would simply collapse. I like this technique for creating more traditional basket shapes as well.

1. I used 12 strips approximately 15 in. long and 36 strips about 7 in. long. Lay out six long strips vertically and start to weave a basic square base, weaving the shorter strips across. Weave a 12 by 12 base, with the long strips going one way and the short strips the other. Even up the ends in both directions and pack a little if the weaving is too loose.

2. On one side of the woven square, you are going to weave another base with the short strips on the long strips just like the first. You will not be weaving it out from the center but from bottom to top, using the previous woven square as a guide. The first strip in the next square will weave

1

2a

2c

2b

3

4c

4a

4d

4b

the exact opposite of the last strip of the one below it. If it was going over 2, then it will be going under 2, etc. Look at the previous base and follow the pattern from the bottom to the top (2a–2c).

3. On finishing that square, turn the weaving 180 degrees and do the same on the other side. You will have three woven squares. Pack the weaving and try to make each square the same size.

4. This gives you three places on each side to do a corner, plus one at each end, for a total of eight corners to weave. I change from one side to the other as I do the corners—I don't weave all the corners on one side, and then the other. It makes for a more uniform structure when you switch from side to side. This also helps bend the woven strip along the lines of where the corners will be, with the corners folded up, and the edge where the squares go together folded down (4a). 4b shows all the bottom corners woven. Weave the end corners (4c); image 4d shows the bottom of the base.

5

6

5. After weaving all the corners, you will have an oblong shape that rests upon the three Vs of the woven base.

6. The woven-up piece.

7. When using this technique, you want the longer weavers to have enough length to do the same amount of weaving up the sides of the basket as the short pieces. I feel it is better to have them a little too long than too short. There is less wastage if the fewer longer pieces are too long, rather than wasting the length of the more numerous short pieces.

You could weave smaller or larger squares, or you could weave the short weavers into rectangles and see how that changes the look of the piece. Use longer center strips and add more squares and consequently more corners.

Another possibility is to weave the center square with two sets of longer strips and then use shorter weavers to weave squares on each of the four arms of the piece. This will create an X or + shaped piece. There are many possibilities with this technique.

Multiple Starts

A lot of my work is created using multiple starts or units to construct a piece. I have found various ways to weave separate pieces together to make a greater whole. You will spend significantly more time packing a multi-start project than a regular piece. The weavers will resist the packing process, because of the angles involved. You just have to be patient and persistent in the packing to get the weavers to go where they need to be.

Multiple Two-Corner Pieces

1. Woven Side to Side

1. I made two two-corner 10 x 10 bases that I wove about half way up the sides.

2. To weave the baskets together, you need to create a space in the side so they can be interwoven in 3/3 twill. I unwove one weaver on the side next to the yellow weaver (**2a**). Next I unwove two of the three weavers that the first piece was originally woven over. They come out under the yellow weaver in an under 1 and under 2, plus a third piece coming under 3. The original unwoven piece, plus the two weavers next to it, is an over 1, over 2, and over 3, creating a V in the weaving (**2b**). This V simulates a corner where you can weave it to another V woven into an additional piece. I will usually attach a clip on each side to keep

the sides of the V separate (**2c**). Create this V in both baskets where you want them to be woven together.

3. Place the two pieces with the Vs face to face where you want to weave them together (**3a**). Because of the unwoven spot, the weavers are ready to continue doing the twill with an over or under 3. Take the weavers from the piece on your right and start weaving them to the piece on your left (**3b** and **3c**). Use clips to keep the weaving together. Weave a few short rows back and forth and pack some as you go.

2c

3b

3a

3c

4a

4b

4c

4d

4e

4. Turn the two pieces so you can now weave the other side together (4a). Weave three or four rows back and forth, with some packing in each connecting section, before you weave the basket to the same height (4b–c). There will be a hole where you wove the two together, but it will get smaller as you pack the weaving. Weave each side until you have all the weavers at the same height (4d–e). You can just weave until you run out of weavers, but you will want to think about shaping the basket first. The separate sections can be tied together or forced apart with spacers.

5a

5b

5. I tied the legs together of one piece with some waste waxed linen in a slightly twisted orientation (5a). I knew that the piece would not stand and would lie on its side (5b).

6. The other piece I wanted to stand, and I used a section of plastic straw to create a spacer tied on with waste waxed linen (6a–b). When doing these structural interventions, I try to do the tying together or adding of spacers on the piece not too long after I have gotten the basket woven all to the same height. While weaving and packing the basket, you want the sections to be where you require them. This will aid in them conforming to the shape you want. If you wait too long before doing your intervention, the basket may not take on the shape that you want. Regardless, there is no guarantee it will. Spacers will usually create distances that stay when removed. Tied-together pieces sometimes will not stay next to each other after the spare thread is removed. If that's the case, I will tie them again with an appropriately colored thread so it is not obvious, and try to tie the threads off so that they do not show. With the size of the separate baskets I started with and weaving them side to side, the pieces look very much like legged torsos.

There are various ways of weaving the
individual sections together. They can be end
to end, side to side, or somewhere in between.
The easiest way is if both pieces are the same
height, but they don't have to be. Both pieces,
however, need to have their outside weavers
going the same direction, either all to the right
or all to the left. You can get some interesting
forms when the pieces are of different heights
or sizes.

You can weave more than two pieces together
either in tandem or in some other shape. You
can use any woven form you wish; it does not
have to be just two corner base pieces. You
can use a square or rectangle pieces or mix
and match. You can use this technique with
any shape of basket done in diagonal twill.

6a

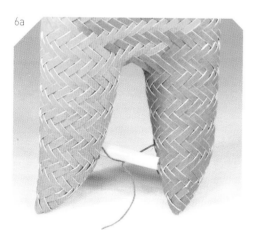

6b

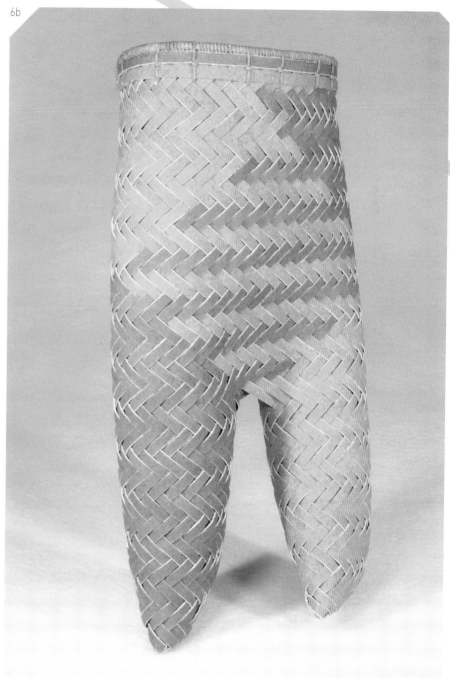

2. Woven Corner to Corner

7. I made three two-corner 10 x 10 bases with just one corner on each piece. I left the other corner unwoven (7a–b). The three unwoven corners will be used to weave the three pieces together. Take one piece and hold it next to another piece, with the unwoven corners at the top (7c). Take the weavers from one side of the corner in one basket, and weave them to one side of the neighboring basket's corner (7d). Follow the process of weaving over 3s one way and weave back by 3s. Pack the weavers as you can and continue weaving until they are all the same height (7e).

7a
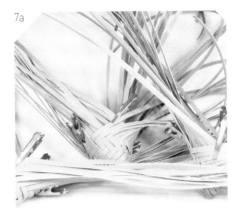

7d

7b

7e
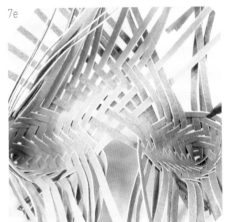

7c

8. Take the third basket and place it next to the first basket, and weave the other half of that corner to the third basket (**8a**). Weave it up with packing, just like the first basket with the second basket (**8b**). You now can weave the third and second basket together, the same as the first and second (**8c**). You will have a hole in the middle of the weaving, but try to make it as small as you can by packing without stressing the weavers too much (**8d**). I usually decide now whether I want the original first three corners to come together (the resulting basket will lie on its side) or stay separate, so they can stand on the points. If you want them to stay together, tie them together with some waxed linen (**8e**).

8a

8d

8b

8e

8c
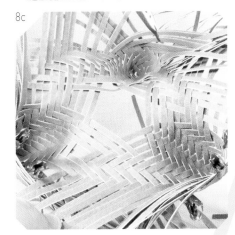

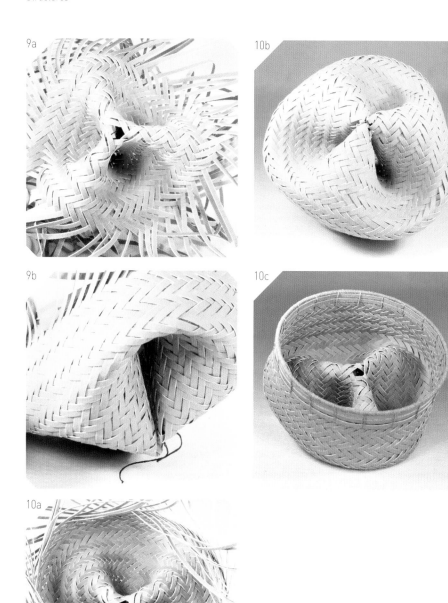

9a

9b

10a

10b

10c

9. I concentrate on packing the work and getting it as evenly woven as possible. I may weave a row or two more before I decide which side I want to be the inside and which side I want to be the outside (9a). I could have kept weaving with the blue on the outside, but I decided that I wanted to switch to the gray. So I started weaving and packing the basket from the gray side, to get it to go up with the blue on the inside (9b). Whichever way I chose, there would be a lot of packing to do! The weaving wants to keep going outward, and you want it to go up. It seems you will never get it to really pack properly, when suddenly it seems you come to an inflection point, and it will start to weave upward more easily.

10. The larger the basket, the longer it seems to take to get to that inflection point. You just have to keep working at it, and it will eventually get easier to pack and weave (10a). After trimming the waste thread from the bottom, I sewed the points together with a near-invisible gray thread (10b). When I finished weaving this piece, it was several inches taller than in the finished image (10c). So I cut about 2 in. off the top of the basket, because I wanted to be able to see more of the inside of the work.

11. I wanted the points to stay apart, so I used some lengths of drinking straw to stabilize the distance between them and to keep them from moving around as I wove the sides (**11a**). After removing the straw spacers, the second piece stands on its points (**11b**).

Note that you can use any unwoven corner in a basket to weave it to any other unwoven corner in another basket—or even in the same basket, if you want that challenge. Two corner bases are not the only choice. You can use any shape of baskets to weave together or mix and match. You can use a corner to weave into another basket by unweaving the side (as in photo 3), which forms a type of corner in the side of the piece.

11a

11b

Multiple Squares to Create Strips

Another technique I use is to make multiple square 3/3 twill woven units and weave them together into a strip. I find this is the easiest method to get a uniform strip, rather than try to keep the angles correct if woven in one continuous piece. I have used these to create Möbius and infinity strips.

I have basket-bombed a tree with one before, just like knitters will place knitted strips around objects such as poles or trees. They could be used as a collar on a basket or in ways I have not thought of yet. A Möbius strip has one twist in it; an infinity strip has two twists. These decisions need to be considered when designing a piece. It is also important to note that the Möbius will have only one continuous rim edge to finish and one continuous surface, while an infinity strip will have two rim edges to finish and two surfaces (sides).

The strip also needs to be long enough to do the twist without too much effort, but not so loose that it loses its structural integrity. You also need some space to work on the rim as it twists around. The wider the strip, the longer it will need to be to accommodate the twist(s).

It does not matter if you are going to create an infinity piece if the two woven sides are a different color or pattern from each other, because when you twist the strip twice, the same sides will be woven together.

A Möbius, on the other hand, has only one twist. One side is woven to the other so you will have a break in the pattern. It will not look continuous unless you plan ahead. I make an odd number of squares with a different color on each, then weave them alternately together. Before the strip is twisted, with an odd number of alternating squares, you will have the same color at each end, but the twist will bring the opposite color up to be woven together. The same process can be used to do an infinity strip; you would use an even number of alternating squares because of the double twist.

The strip can also be twisted more than one or two times; it just needs to be long enough to accommodate more twists. Keep in mind that an even number of twists will give you two rims and two surfaces like an infinity strip, and an odd number of twists will give you only one rim and one continuous surface like a Möbius.

Left: "Ocher Möbius."

1a

1b

1c

1. All these units are 9 x 9 (3/3 twill squares). You want to start each square the same way so that you can weave them all together (**1a**). It doesn't matter how you start them; it only matters that they are all woven the same. The square will be woven together end to end, but they need to be with the Vs running left to right, not top to bottom (**1b**). You have to make sure that you have the two ends together that have complementary weaving patterns so you can weave the 3/3 twill. The photo shows them in the correct orientation to weave together. Your woven squares may not look like these two, which doesn't matter as long as they will weave together in pattern (**1c**). If they don't look like they will weave together properly, try the other end of one of the two squares. If it still does not look like you can weave them together in the 3/3 pattern, you may not have woven the squares in the same way, or you may just be having difficulty seeing the pattern. Check to see that you have woven your squares the same way.

2. Once you have the squares oriented properly, you can start weaving them together (**2a**). You will need to work to get the squares closely woven together (**2b**). Completely weave each square to each other (**2c**). Continue to add more squares (**2d**).

3. To weave a Möbius strip, use an odd number of squares so the pattern will be correct after the one twist. I wove 13 squares into a strip (**3a**). The ends before they are twisted (**3b**). The ends after twisting once (**3c**). I began weaving the ends together to form a Möbius strip. Because of the single twist, the two ends will not simply weave together as they will in the infinity strip with its two twists. With one twist the weave pattern is not in alignment, so you cannot weave the two ends together in the basic 3/3 twill. The ends will have to be woven together in a broken twill pattern. Where the two squares weave together, the edge weavers will weave the opposite of each other. If one is over 3, the other will be under 3, for example (**3d**). This will create a line of 1, 2, and 3 just like in the four-cornered broken twill base (**3e**).

3a

3b

3c

3d

3e

The Möbius before being trimmed (**3f**). Edges trimmed and the rim pieces added. If you look closely, you can see that there is only one rim edge on this piece (**3g**).

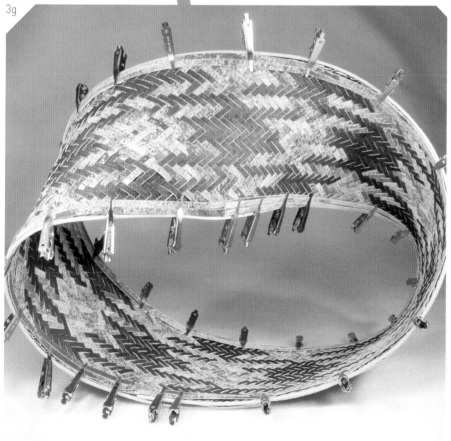

4. To weave an infinity loop, use an even number of squares so the pattern will be correct after the two twists. I wove 14 squares into a strip (4a). The two ends before and after twisting (4b and 4c).

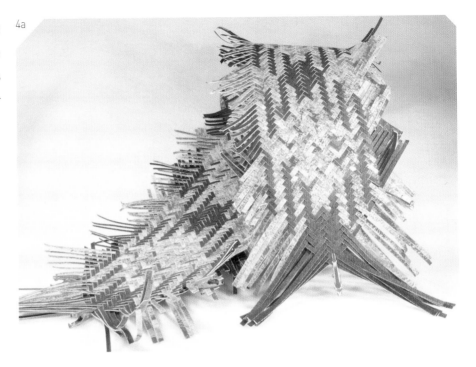

4a

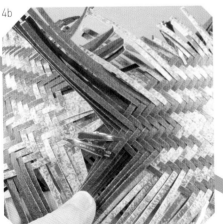

4b

4c

4d

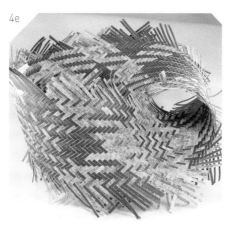

4e

The two ends woven together (4d). The two twists allow the weaving in the end squares to be in alignment to weave together in 3/3 twill. The piece all woven together before being trimmed (4e). Trimmed and one set of rim pieces added. The second set of rim pieces has not been added yet, instead showing the two rim edges on this piece (4f).

4f

Color Patterns

The following are examples of base patterns and how they look after they are woven. I worked these up on fairly small bases with just two colors. The possible patterns that can be worked on larger bases, using more spokes and colors, are endless. I recommend you play around with other possibilities to see what you can discover.

Patterns 1 through 7

These were created with paper painted a different solid color on each side and using the four-corner square base.

1. Start this pattern with one of one color and two of the second color, repeated out in each direction from the center. Each side is the opposite in color of the other side. I chose to weave up the side with the double blacks. You will get a zigzag or lightning look that goes straight up the side. This was done with an 18 x 18 base.

2. This pattern is woven with each of the colors alternating one by one. The reverse-side colors will be the opposite, but the woven pattern will essentially be the same on both sides. This also gives a zigzag, but the design runs to the left. This is a pattern where you need to take into consideration what the color of the last weaver is in comparison with the center colored weavers. You need to weave this pattern with an even number of sets of three weavers, so you do not have a double line of the same color. This was done with a 24 x 24 base.

1a

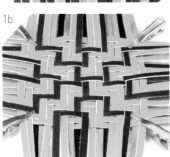
1b

1c

2a

2b

3. The same as in pattern #2, but I used an odd number of weaver sets. The pattern becomes broken and you do not get a continuous zigzag. This creates an interesting look as well. This was woven with an 18 x 18 base.

3a

3b

4. For this pattern, start weaving with two of one color and one of the second color, repeated out in each direction from the center. Each side is the opposite in color of the reverse. I chose to weave up the side with the double blacks. It gives the piece what I call a windowpane effect of one color surrounded by the other color. Herringbone may be a better name. This was done with an 18 x 18 base.

4a

4b

4c

5. All the same colors go in each direction with this pattern: one color only vertical and the other color all horizontal when you are looking at the base. When woven up, it creates alternating diamond shapes of the single colors and mixed-color diamonds.

    In a 3/3 twill, to get the best-looking diamonds, you need to use a number divisible by nine, which is the square of three. This base is 18 x 18 weavers, or nine weavers from the center on each side. If you are doing a different twill number, to get the best diamond you need a number divided by the square of the twill. If you were doing 2/2 twill, you need a number divisible by four. If doing a 4/4 twill, you would need a number divisible by 16.

5a

5b

6. In this base pattern I wove out each side from the center, half and half of each color. This creates two solid-color squares opposite each other and two mixed-color squares. This weaves up with diamonds twice as large (18 x 18) as in pattern 5. This was done with an 18 x 18 base.

6a

6b

7. This starts the same as # 6, but I switched colors after nine strips to the opposite. The sides weave into large and small diamonds, and rectangles. This was done with a 36 x 36 base.

7a

7b

Patterns 8 through 10

These were created with paper painted a different solid color on each side and using the two-corner base.

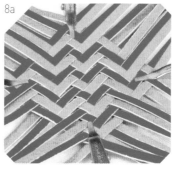
8a

8b

8. This is a pattern of two alternating colors on a two-corner base. The piece on the corner weaves back on itself, so it will double up the color when woven up in the basket. Because the color gets doubled at the corner, you get a broken pattern of zigzag stripes up the basket. You need to consider the doubling of the color on the ends when designing a pattern using the two-corner base. This was done with a 12 x 12 base.

9. This pattern takes into account that the end weavers double back on each other. The pattern is one weaver of one color and two weavers of the other color. For the pattern to work, each single end weaver should be thought of as being the same as two weavers in terms of the color.

This pattern was woven one red, one yellow, two red, one yellow, two reds, one yellow, two reds, one yellow, and one red. The colors were the opposite of the other side, and I decided to weave it with the predominantly yellow side out. This makes a zigzag pattern as in pattern number 1. This was done with a 12 x 12 base.

9a 9b

10. This base looks deceptively like the one in #9, but to get the pattern on the sides you need to do two strokes of 2/2 twill, then switch to 3/3 twill. If you look closely at the second image, you will see that from the over 1, it goes under 2 and over 2, then starts the 3/3 twill. On a base this small it is harder to see, because many of the weavers are weaving one and two at the edge. So to get the same look as in pattern #4, you have to weave one set of 2/2 twill from the over/under 1 center and do 3/3 twill from there on. When doing the corners it is the same—you have to weave the 2/2 pattern at first before doing the 3/3. This was done with a 12 x 12 base.

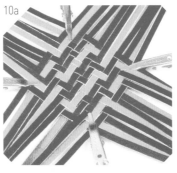
10a 10c

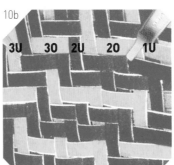
10b
3U 3O 2U 2O 1U

Patterns 11 through 14

These were created with paper that had been divided in half on one side, with each half painted a different solid color and using the four-corner square base (I painted the other side black). The colors will change from one to the other at the centerline or where the twill breaks. You want to try to keep the change of color hidden under the weaving along the centerline.

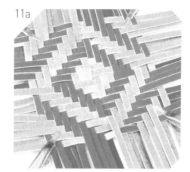

11a

11b

11. This base is woven so that the weaver's colors are oriented the same on each side around the base. It is blue, then orange, all around the base: the colors are the opposite of each other on each side. This is the only pattern that I know of on this type of base that will create the horizontal bands of color on the sides. From the center out at the top, all the weavers are orange to the right of center and the blue is to the left. As you turn the base this orientation is the same. This was done with an 18 x 18 base.

12. This base is woven so the two colors are solid blocks of color in each corner. When woven up, they create the diamond pattern on the sides. This was done with an 18 x 18 base.

12a

12b

13. This base starts the same as pattern #12, but you switch the directions the colors are woven to get another solid-color square at the corners and intermixed squares in the middle. This creates large diamonds on the side of the basket. This was done with a 36 x 36 base.

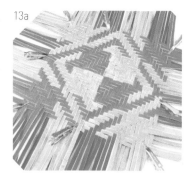

If you weave a larger base and you want the small diamonds on the sides, versus larger diamonds, you need to have the solid-color squares on the base to occur where you are going to weave the corners. If you want the larger diamonds, the mixed-color squares need to be where the corners will be woven. If you wanted to do three repeats of the colors alternating on the base, you start with the solid colors for the small diamonds. For the larger diamonds, you start with mixed-color squares.

14. This alternates a two/one pattern of color placement. As you weave in two strips, they will be blue on one half of the base and orange on the other. The next single strip will be orange, then blue on the other half of the base. Continue that pattern all around the base. This creates a zigzag pattern going straight up the basket. It looks very similar to pattern #1, but each stripe is actually two and one strip wide: in pattern #1, each stripe is either two weavers wide or one weaver wide, not intermixed.

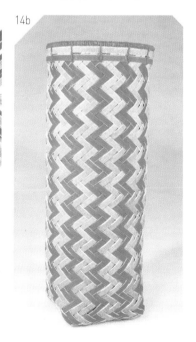

Patterns 15 and 16

These were created with paper that was divided in half on one side, with each half painted a different solid color and using the two-corner base. You want the color change to happen along the centerline of under 1s.

15. This is done by weaving all one color in one direction, with the change in color of the two color strips along the centerline. When woven up, you get alternating diamonds. This was done with a 12 x 12 base.

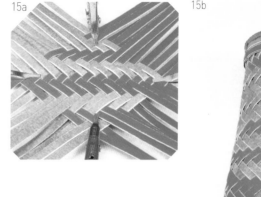

16. This alternates the colors in each direction along the centerline. You do not have a problem with the outside pieces doubling up the color, because each end is a different color. When woven up you get zigzag stripes. This was done with a 12 x 12 base.

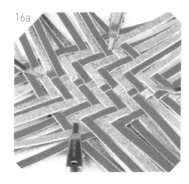

Correcting Common Problems

Errors in the Base Twill

You can find errors when you are weaving your base at any time—most likely when you are packing the base. To correct an error in your weaving, you need, preferably, a flat awl to gently unweave the piece that is woven incorrectly. You can break the weaver while doing this, so be careful while unweaving and then reweaving the piece back in. This is a little harder to do if you have already packed the base tight. So check the weaving for possible errors before packing, if possible.

1. The arrow indicates the error.

2. Gently pull the weaver out of the woven section with an awl.

3. The weaver is completely unwoven up to the error.

4. Starting to reweave the piece correctly.

5. Almost completely woven back.

6. The correction is done and the reweaving is complete.

Unwanted Color Showing on Double-Colored Base

Sometimes after you have finished a base with the bi-color weavers, you will find some spots where the other color shows where it should not. It is usually just a little, and you may not mind since it is the base of the basket, so it will not show. However, if you want to correct it, you can sometimes just carefully pull the weaver a little bit to hide the off color under the weaver, provided the base has not been packed yet. This is easiest on the weavers toward the outside edge.

1. The error.

2. On a larger base, even if it is not yet packed, it will be difficult to pull a piece without breaking it because of the amount of friction this will create. To correct without damaging the weaver, go to the outside edge on the correct side of the base where the color is showing, and pull up a little bit of the weaver with an awl.

3. Pull the slack up in the next spot and continue to take up the slack at each over weaver, until you reach the center and the wrong color slides under and is hidden (3a–3c).

4. Continue to take up the slack in the weaver all the way to the other side of the base. When you create the slack you want, it should be just enough to correct the placement of the weaver, but not so much that it may be too far the other way. If it is not enough or too much, just repeat the process again until it looks correct.

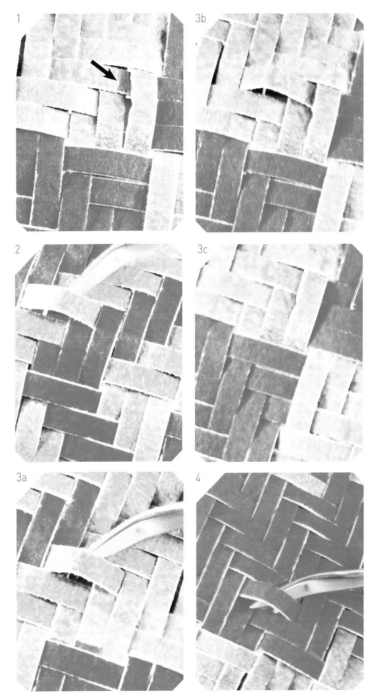

1

4

2

5

3

6

Short Weaver

Sometimes a weaver breaks; sometimes one may be too short if the weavers were not evened out at the beginning. If you need to add to an existing weaver, follow this procedure.

1. Take a spare weaver and cut a point in one end to make it easier to thread into the basket.

2. Use a flat awl to gently open a space under a set of three weavers, and run the new piece over the short piece.

3. Weave it under another set of three.

4. Finish pulling the new weaver through.

5. I leave about a 0.5 in. or so tail.

6. Finish up the basket, weaving the old and new pieces together until the old piece runs out.

   I usually don't trim the tail until I've finished the basket. I give a little pull on the tail as I cut it off as close to the side as I can with some snips. Sometimes you will have a tail on the inside, as well, from the short weaver, but mostly it's not noticeable.

Errors When Weaving the Sides of the Basket

Errors in the twill on the sides of the basket are usually caught pretty quickly, particularly when you do the packing on the sides. They are easy to correct since they are usually only a row or two below where you are working.

1. The errors are usually an over 2 or 4.

2. Or occasionally you will have a couple of neighboring spokes that have been woven in the wrong order.

3. If you find an error, you can unweave the area of the basket that is wrong and reweave it correctly. You can also just pull the one or two pieces out (*3a–3d*).

4. And correct the weaving error by reweaving them correctly.

1

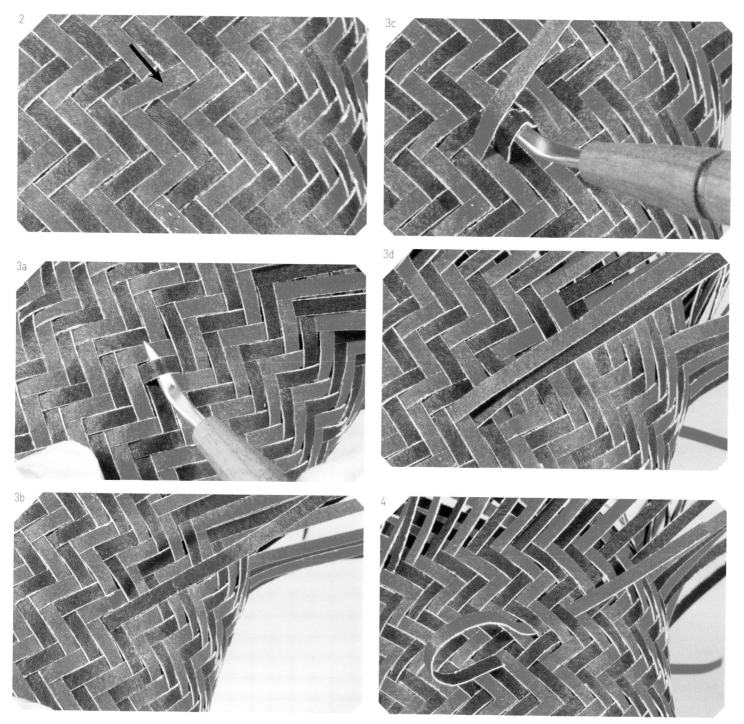

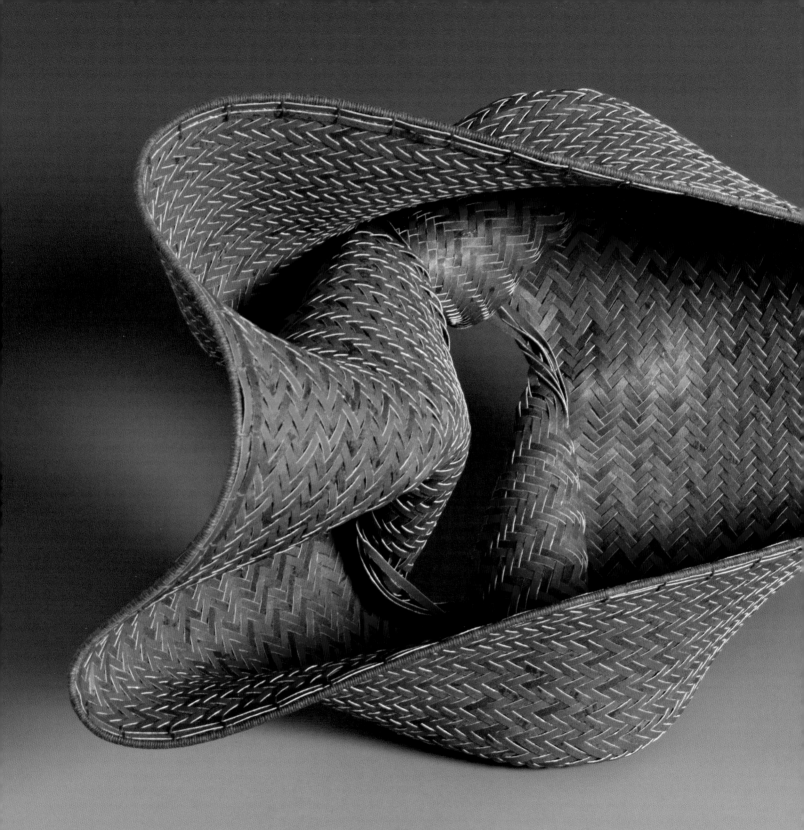

Exploring Concepts

I believe it is a really good practice to keep some kind of journal or sketchbook to record ideas—whether in words or drawings. I have kept an ideas journal—an 8 x 5 in. spiral-bound sketchbook—for 30 years now. I mostly keep it beside my bed, since I often have many ideas before I fall asleep: if I don't write the ideas down, they have a tendency to keep me awake. If I get the idea down on paper, I also do not have to worry that I might not remember it later.

Occasionally, I need to write something down on loose paper because I don't have my book with me. I'll later staple the sheet into the book so it doesn't get lost in a pile of papers somewhere. I'm on my fifth book now!

There can be long stretches of time when I don't write much in the journal, and other times there will be periods of constant noting of ideas and concepts. I'll never have time to do all the ideas I've written down, but the ideas are always available to review if I am looking for some inspiration or a new direction to explore.

Previous page: "Displacement," photo by Ken Rowe.

"Möbius 2."
The following pages show some of my weaving explorations to do with mathematical solids. All photos in this section, unless specified, were taken by Ken Rowe.

"Pythagoras 1."
An interpretation of a right-angle triangle using the Pythagorean theorem.

"Pythagoras 2."

An interpretation of the geometric proof of the Pythagorean theorem.

I find there are a lot of possible inspirations for work in the world. Even though I am a process-driven artist and do not create much in the way of conceptual work, I find a lot of my ideas in math and geometry. I use my inspirations as a way to create new processes or techniques that will allow me to create the imagined work.

I have played with Möbius and infinity strips. I have created a couple of pieces based on Pythagoras's hypotenuse theorem $(a^2 + b^2 = c^2)$ and have been inspired by three-dimensional solids.

I have been working on a series of Platonic solid pieces. A Platonic solid is where each face is the same regular polygon, and the same number of polygons meet at each vertex (or corner). A cube (hexahedron) is a Platonic solid.

There are only five Platonic solids: the tetrahedron (four triangular faces), hexahedron (six square faces), octahedron (eight triangular faces), dodecahedron (12 pentagonal faces), and icosahedron (20 triangular faces). I have finished my first versions of the Platonic solids and have started on the second and third series, exploring the shapes further. I also have thoughts on how to do a fourth variation. Each iteration uses a different technique or variation to create a unique look to each set.

Once I finish the Platonic solids, there are still the Archimedean and Johnson solids, which respectively have 13 and 92 variations. There are also a whole host of prisms and antiprisms to consider.

"Hexahedron."
For my hexahedron Platonic solid, I wove together six four-sided starts.

"Tetrehedron."
I wove together four three-sided starts to create a tetrahedron Platonic solid.

"Hexahedron 2."
*I wove together 12
stair step strips to
create this hexahedron
Platonic solid.*

"Tetrahedron 3."
*Four three-legged
starts were woven to
create this tetrahedron
Platonic solid.*

I have always been interested in creating a "Klein basket"—an idea inspired by the Klein bottle. A Klein bottle has only one surface. Like the Möbius strip, it's a three-dimensional representation of a four-dimensional object. I plan on designing and weaving a Klein basket one day. There are also the Möbius ladder and Möbius torus to explore.

I have done work using the Fibonacci sequence, which is a series of numbers that are created by adding the two numbers next to each other to create the next one in the sequence: 0,1, 1, 2, 3, 5, 8, 13, 21, 34, etc. I have also looked at fractals and Koch snowflakes, which are a type of fractal.

I recently came across the idea of using algebraic expressions in my baskets, based on *Algebraic Expressions in Handwoven Textiles* by Ada Dietz. This monograph defines and creates loom-weaving patterns based on the expansion of multivariate polynomials. An example is $(x-y)^2$ becomes x^2 - 2xy - y2, then to xx xy xy yy or xxx yx yyy. I am not certain how I will incorporate the use of algebraic expressions into my work, but I believe I'll use it at some future date.

I have files on various means of non-verbal communication, such as Braille and Morse code, which I feel would translate well into some basketry techniques.

I have looked at semaphore, international maritime signal flags, and the phonetic military alphabet as possible stimuli to new work. I have even looked at the names of old British money and hereditary titles. I have files on the Greek alphabet, full-moon names, and names for animal groupings.

I collect possible ideas for projects that I find online in a folder on my computer, or I bookmark them in my favorites list.

I have considered how to represent the particles in the standard model of physics. These include fermions consisting of six leptons and six quarks and the four bosons. The quarks have interesting names, which are up, down, charm, strange, top, and bottom. I have thought about how to represent those names, but have not come up with a definitive plan yet. I have considered the atom and the periodic table, as well, for possible ideas.

These are just some of the places my mind has wandered through over the years. There are so many ways to find inspiration in the world. If you are

"Octahedron."
Eight three-sided starts created my octahedron Platonic solid.

"Dodecahedron."
I wove together 12 five-sided starts to create a dodecahedron Platonic solid.

"Icosahedron."
I wove together 20 three-sided starts to create an icosahedron Platonic solid.

"Gold and Lavender Fibonacci." *This piece used the Fibonacci sequence 1, 2, 3, 5, 8, 13, 21. Each color shows the sequence in opposite directions, so 1 gold (G), 21 lavender (L), 1 G, 13L, 2G, 8L, 3G, 5L, 5G, 3L, 8G,2L, 13G, 1L, 21G, 1L. (Author)*

interested in plants or flowers, I am certain there are ways to use that interest to spur your muse. If you are interested in music, another form of math, there are numerous areas to explore.

I believe that any area of interest a person may have can inspire their artwork, whether they are a conceptual artist or a process-driven artist. From astronomy to zoology, I believe there is always some way to interpret the information of your interest into a basket. Other crafts may stimulate you as well—quilting or knitting may trigger some new ideas. Taking classes in a variety of different basket techniques, styles, and materials, or with various instructors, is a good way to open your mind to new possibilities.

I believe that everything I learn can, and does, inform my art in some way or another.

Color is a whole other area to explore. Monochromatic colors, bold juxtapositions of colors, or gradations of color are all possibilities for inspiration.

You can play with the size of the weavers to create different looks using the same techniques. You could try weaving anything, from miniatures to human size to room installations. A piece can be made from several works that are grouped together or perhaps sit inside one another. Definitely try working in series to flesh out ideas or see where a certain process will take you.

When you make your work, keep another book to record information about each piece: how you constructed it, the materials you used, etc. This will allow you to recreate a piece or something similar without having to start from scratch. Maybe include your thoughts about or inspiration for the piece. Perhaps keep track of the time involved in weaving the work. I usually record my time, the date I finish the piece, the title, and the finished size, among other things.

"Red and Black Fibonacci."

This Fibonacci sequence in basketry: 1, 2, 3, 5, 8, with alternating colors (1B, 8R, 1B, 5R, 2B, 3R, 3B, 2R, 5B, 1R, 8B, 1R. (Author)

Don't be afraid to try out new ideas or to take leaps into new areas. If something does not work, it will likely send you in another direction that will produce something you'll find interesting. Even your failures are informative.

Sometimes you want to force the work to go in a particular direction that it may not really want to go. Let go of your preconceived ideas and let the work go where it naturally wants to evolve.

Also, be aware that you are your own worst critic. The flaws you see in your work will not be seen or even noticed by people looking at the work: they are seeing the whole piece, not individual details of the work.

I find looking at other basketmakers' work or other artists' work can be another source of inspiration. Not to copy their work, but to maybe see shapes, processes, color, or other aspects of the work that may stimulate new creative ideas. I have bookmarked several artists' websites whose work intrigues me and makes me think of new possibilities in my own work.

"Pink and Gray Fibonacci."
As with the gold and lavender piece, the colors of this piece each show a Fibonacci sequence in opposite directions, so 1 pink (P), 21 gray (G), 1P, 13G, 2P, 8G, 3P, 5G, 5P, 3G, 8P, 2G, 13P, 1G, 21P, 1G. (Jerry McCollum)

Acknowledgments

I would like to thank R. Leon Russell and Wilma Ziegler for their invaluable editing skills. I would also like to thank my sister Anne and the friends and family who encouraged me in this endeavor.

Resources

Supplies

Dick Blick Art Supplies   dickblick.com

Jerry's Artarama   jerrysartarrama.com

Radio Schack   radioschack.com

Royalwood   royalwoodltd.com

Basket Maker's Catalog   basketmakerscatalog.com

Rumi Sumaq   rumisumaq.com

Fante's Kitchen Shop   fantes.com

Organizations

Northwest Basket Weavers   nwbasketweavers.org

Northwest Designer Craftsmen   nwdesignercraftsmen.org

National Basketry Organization   nationalbasketry.org

Handweavers Guild of America   weavespindye.org

Surface Design Association   surfacedesign.org

Fiber Art Now   fiberartnow.net

American Craft Magazine   craftcouncil.org

About the Author

Dorothy McGuinness has been weaving sculptural baskets using diagonal twill techniques for over 20 years. She utilizes watercolor paper and acrylic paints as her medium of choice. She has gathered extensive basketry knowledge from over 30 years of learning and exploring the various weaving methods that have been handed down through the ages. Dorothy has participated in numerous local, national, and international shows and has won various national and international awards. What most attracts Dorothy to using paper and paint for weaving is the ability to play with color and pattern. She enjoys exploring the interplay of weaving, color, and design in new sculptural pieces and continues to experiment. Dorothy was born in 1961 in western Washington and currently resides in Everett, Washington. dorothymmcguinness.com